Barbarians to Bureaucrats

Corporate Life Cycle Strategies

Lessons from the Rise and Fall of Civilizations

by Lawrence M. Miller

Fawcett Columbine • New York

A Fawcett Columbine Book
Published by Ballantine Books

Library of Congress Catalog Card Number:
89-91508

ISBN: 978-0-449-90526-5

This edition published by arrangement with Clarkson
N. Potter, Inc., New York

Cover design by James R. Harris

Manufactured in the United States of America

16

Contents

ACKNOWLEDGMENTS
PAGE vii

INTRODUCTION
PAGE 1

STAGE 1
The Prophet: Inspiration and Innovation
PAGE 9

STAGE 2
The Barbarian: Crisis and Conquest
PAGE 34

STAGE 3
The Builder and Explorer: Specialization and Expansion
PAGE 59

STAGE 4
The Administrator: Systems, Structure, and Security
PAGE 83

STAGE 5
The Bureaucrat: The Tight Grip of Control
PAGE 110

STAGE 6
The Aristocrat: Alienation and Revolution
PAGE 139

STAGE 7
The Synergist Prescription
PAGE 165

MANAGING COMPETITIVE STRATEGY WITHIN
PAGE 192

A LIFE CYCLE OVERVIEW
PAGE 216

NOTES AND REFERENCES
PAGE 223

INDEX
PAGE 227

Acknowledgments

I t is only because of my partners and associates that I have been able to write this book. I am in debt to Jennifer Howard, Tom Werner, and Bob Lynch, who have so expertly carried on the work of our consulting firm, giving me the peace of mind to concentrate on this task. Jeanne Ann McDaniel has been the most competent and cheerful of office managers, assuring some order in my administrative affairs.

During the past several years my speaking agents, Joe and Janet Cosby of the Cosby Bureau International in Washington, D.C., have become good friends and have been a continual source of encouragement and support. Equally important, they have provided many opportunities to share my ideas with audiences throughout the country, allowing me to refine my presentations.

I am especially grateful to Randa Wilbur, who first encouraged me to write this book and who provided valuable input. Catherine Rowell, Steve Rexford, William "Buck" Tuppeny, and Bonnie Barnes also gave me helpful comments.

I am certain that without the encouragement and continual support of Margaret McBride, my very patient and persistent literary agent, this book would never have been written. And I am grateful to my editor, Carol Southern, for her tenacity, precise critiques, and good cheer. Paul Brown also provided invaluable editing and assistance in the final rewrite.

And, finally, I must thank my family, who has tolerated seemingly endless periods of obsessive hibernation, the only condition under which I know how to write; my deepest gratitude to my wife, Carole, and my children, Langdon, Natasha, and Layli.

—L.M.M.

Introduction

All living things, whether plants, animals, people or groups of people, exhibit patterns or cycles of development, moving from periods of vitality and growth, to periods of decay and disintegration. The pattern of business growth and decline—and the behavior of leaders—follows this same course.

In this book I present a theory of corporate life cycles. With it comes an explanation for the natural stages of evolution of the company and its leaders as they confront the challenges they are most likely to face as the company matures. This theory is derived from a study of leadership throughout human history and provides an explanation for bureaucratization and the alienation of leadership in our government and society. The conclusion to this theory is the Law of Synergy, which, I believe, offers the hope of harnessing both

1

the spiritual and material assets of the corporation or society. By breaking the cyclical pattern, leaders can advance the corporation or the culture to ever more vital growth and development.

I have identified seven stages of corporate life and seven leadership styles that dominate during each stage:

1. The Prophet: The visionary who creates the breakthrough and the human energy to propel the company forward.

2. The Barbarian: The leader of crisis and conquest who commands the corporation on the march of rapid growth.

3. The Builder and Explorer: The developers of the specialized skills and structures required for growth, who shift from command to collaboration.

4. The Administrator: The creator of the integrating system and structure, who shifts the focus from expansion to security.

5. The Bureaucrat: The imposer of a tight grip of control, who crucifies and exiles new prophets and barbarians, assuring the loss of creativity and expansion.

6. The Aristocrat: The inheritor of wealth, alienated from those who do productive work, who is the cause of rebellion and disintegration.

7. The Synergist: The leader who maintains the balance, who continues the forward motion of a large and complex structure by unifying and appreciating the diverse contribution of the Prophet, Barbarian, Builder, Explorer, and Administrator.

At each stage and for each leadership style, challenges inevitably develop. During growth, leaders respond creatively to challenge. During decline, they respond mechanically, relying on responses that have been successful in the past. Both cultures and companies continue to progress so long as leaders recognize the challenges and respond creatively. Each successful response leads not to a condition of ease, but to a higher level of challenge requiring yet another new and creative response. Creative response is the essential function of leaders. The moment leaders relax and rely on yesterday's successful response in the presence of today's challenge, the decline begins. It is natural for leaders in every stage to rely on responses they find most comfortable and to fail when they do not adopt innovative responses. Both the history of civilizations and of corporations demonstrate this relationship, between the behavior of leaders and the cycle of growth and decline.

And it is the behavior of leaders that explains the dynamic energy, the heroic creation of jobs and wealth created in small, growing businesses, as well as the mess of bureaucracy, the disillusionment and waste of human and capital resources in the uncreative hulk of large corporations and government. It is also the behavior of leaders that forcefully regenerates the company in decline.

Oswald Spengler was among the first to document the stages and styles in world history. He wrote eloquently of the wavelike patterns of civilization:

> Over the expanse of the water passes the endless uniform wave-train of the generations. . . . But over this surface, too, the great Cultures accomplish their majestic wave-cycles. They appear suddenly, swell in splendid lines, flatten again and vanish, and the face of the waters is once more a sleeping waste.[1]

But it is from the work of historian Arnold Toynbee that I have derived greatest inspiration. The thoroughness and insight of his study are without parallel.

The cyclical pattern has also been observed in the life of the great powers throughout history. Paul Kennedy describes the "process of rise and fall among the Great Powers—of differentials in growth rates and technological change, leading to shifts in the global economic balances, which in turn gradually impinge upon the political and military balances."[2] It is the interaction of the internal economy and the society's external influence that is the primary theme of his analysis.

The failure of leadership in the corporation, as well as in the great power, is often a consequence of a failure to understand the relationship between the internal strength of the society and the ability to exert external influence. Leadership is deceived because the society dominates huge territory and is able to exert greater material force than its competition; while at the same time it is losing its internal powers, assuring its eventual loss of external power. This is the historic trap. The internal power of the great power is derived from its relative economic capacity. The external power, as described by Kennedy, is its military power. In the corporation the internal power is the creativity of people, the strength of social purpose, the development of competence, and the ability of its members to act with unified and determined effort. The external power of the corporation is its ability to capture and hold market territory, to dominate the competition, and to strengthen its material resources.

Arthur M. Schlesinger, in his book *The Cycles of American History,* has noted "a continuing shift in national involvement, between public purpose and private interests."[3] There are two sides to his turning wheel. One side is the more personal, even selfish, interest, the freedom to pursue and protect private property, to maximize profits. The second side, which gains ascendancy as the first descends, is the interest in the collective good, social responsibility, and altruism. Unlike the cycles of civilization, each of which builds upon the past and seems to move in a forward motion. Schlesinger's turns of the wheel repeat the same pattern.

This pattern of alternating concerns is also found within the society of a corporation. The wheel turns from the emphasis on the human problems and the material pursuits, the concern for the needs and satisfaction of employees and public, to the need for profits. But, as one observes this pattern, both in the corporation and the civilization, one recognizes that there is a necessary order between the two. "In the beginning was the Word"—the idea, the spirit, precedes the acquisition of the material; but, as material wealth and size are gained, the focus shifts. As the energies turn away from the creative spirit and become excessively focused on that which is material, the power to regenerate, to move forward, vanishes, leaving the uncreative hulk.

The life cycle is not a form of cultural predestination. I believe in free will and the capacity of man to determine his own destiny. However, understanding the various stages within the cycle is useful for the corporate leader for the very reason that the corporation's destiny is very much in his (or her) hands, able to be shaped by effective leadership. By understanding the cycles, managers will become sensitive to both the spiritual and material forces at work within the corporation.

By studying the cycles you will find an explanation for your own company's past creativity and success, current leadership style and organization, and predictions about its future failure. You will also learn to identify the challenges and traps that must be overcome at each stage.

Perhaps you may even recognize your own personality and those of your superiors or your staff and gain some insight into how to become a more effective leader.

This book does not present a simplistic prescription for management nirvana. While I have distilled the lessons of cultural life cycles into nine axioms that I believe summarize the keys to maintaining vitality and upward momentum, studying these maxims is not enough. It is equally important to understand that in different parts of a company's life cycle, different management styles are needed. There is a time to be tough and commanding. There is a time for consensus. There is a time for increasing specialization, and there is another for simplifying the organization. There is a time when the organization is creative and takes risks and another when its leaders seek security. And, perhaps most important, there is a time when the organization must be revitalized, pulled back from its natural tendency to decay.

This is a book about the legitimate differences in corporate culture and leadership. Most writers have argued for a corporate culture they assume to be best for all organizations at all times. Managers know better. They know leadership is situational.

The truly excellent manager can act in many different ways, depending on the situation he faces. In the following pages, each of the life cycle stages is described in terms of a leadership style that is needed at a particular time: Prophet, Barbarian, Builder, Explorer, Administrator, Bureaucrat, Aristocrat, and Synergist. As managers, we tend more toward one style than another and may be most comfortable in a corporation whose stage of development is most compatible with our own. We are also likely to impose our style on an organization whether or not it is the one most needed at that time. This is a common cause of leadership failure.

It is unlikely that any manager perfectly fits the description of one style. It is also unlikely that a company will fit perfectly into the description of one stage. We are more complex. We are capable of change, altering our style as we develop and as our organization changes. When reading these descriptions, try not to pigeonhole individuals or companies. They are likely to be a blend of several, maybe in flux or in the process of change.

Throughout this book I will be making reference to the life cycle curve, describing the organization as it progresses through a natural process of growth and decline.

THE CORPORATE LIFE CYCLE

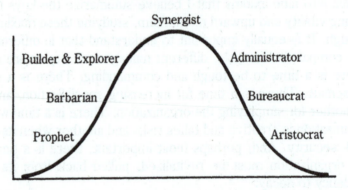

The vertical axis shows the health of the culture as measured by its ability to create new, and maintain present, wealth. By wealth, I do not mean what it takes to make one person, or group of people, rich. Rather, I refer to true wealth, the aggregate of goods and services produced relative to the input. On a national scale, our wealth is the sum of the goods and services produced per capita.

The horizontal axis represents the maturing of the corporation over time.

It is important to make the distinction between the growth or decline of material assets and the development or decline of the culture. They are not one and the same. Indeed, they can move in opposite directions. It is possible for a culture to become creative while its material assets are declining; this growth in creative and dynamic energy is a predictor of future growth in material assets.

Conversely, a loss of creative energy is the most obvious characteristic of decline. And it is creativity—innovation in both products and ways of gaining productivity and quality—that determines competitive success. As we will see, history teaches that leadership must be creative if the organization is to be creative. Leaders must also remain close to their troops, unifying and creating common social purpose. When leaders become alienated from their followers, there is a loss of social unity and creativity. Competitors then attack. This is true of both companies and countries.

CULTURE TO ASSETS CURVE

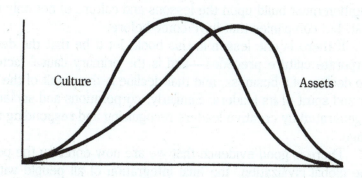

To understand the path of emergence and decline is to understand the interplay of the material and spiritual worlds. During the early period the spiritual energy is high, but material assets few. It appears almost inevitable as the material assets rise that the spiritual will decline. But it is only in the failure to understand and deal with this law that its outcome is so determined.

In his discussion of the interplay of religion and civilization, Arnold Toynbee wrote:

The successive rises and falls of the primary and secondary civilizations are an example of a rhythm—observed in other contexts—in which the successive revolutions of a wheel carry a vehicle, not on the repetitive circular course that the revolving wheel itself describes, but in a progressive movement towards a goal.[4]

He describes that goal as the upward spiral of the spiritual progress of mankind.

Similarly, the successive cycles of corporate life may be viewed as more than the mere rise and fall of the material structure of the corporation. Rather, it may be viewed as the vehicle that, through its very decline, provides the impetus for successive and even greater leaps up the slope of mankind's progress, the process of creating collective wealth and social integration of our society. The growth of a civilization is a process of synergy among people with diverse ideas and beliefs, and each succeeding civilization draws the circle larger than the previous one. So, too, each succeeding corporation must build upon the lessons and culture of not only its own past, but companies that have come before.

If there is one lesson in this book, let it be that the decline in corporate culture precedes—and is the primary causal factor in— the decline of a business, and that decline is the result of the behavior and spirit of its leaders. Similarly, corporations and societies are regenerated by creative leaders recognizing and responding to challenge.

There is good evidence that we are now entering the period of one global civilization, the final integration of all people with their diversity of ideas, energy, and economies. If this is so, the cycle of rise and fall may be broken to be replaced by a global synergy of cultures. In like manner, with a similar synergy of ideas, characteristics, and cultures, it may be possible that the corporation itself will achieve that delicate balance between the creative, which is the source of new wealth, and the administrative order that represents sanity and security. That is our goal.

◆

The Prophet

Inspiration and Innovation

Reasonable men adapt themselves to their environment; un-reasonable men try to adapt their environment to themselves. Thus all progress is the result of the efforts of unreasonable men.

—GEORGE BERNARD SHAW

No one can possibly achieve any real and lasting success or "get rich" in business by being a conformist.

—J. PAUL GETTY

The history of civilizations and corporations reveals a common pattern. Both are formed by the creative force of one person or a small group of people. These founders possess a vision. An idea that is exciting and unique—often one that others thought impossible to achieve. An idea that eventually mobilizes others.

It is the role of the Prophet to develop the idea, the vision of the future. By doing so, he stimulates the energy and creativity of those who follow.

In our materialistic world it is easy to forget that creativity is a spiritual event. The emergence of something new goes beyond sight, touch, and cost-benefit analysis. Nothing is more material than the grandeur of civilizations, but it begins with creative spirit. Oswald Spengler in *The Decline of the West* recognized this:

> A culture is born in the moment when a great soul awakens out of the proto-spirituality of ever-childish humanity. . . . But its living existence, that sequence of great epochs which define and display the stages of fulfilment, is an inner passionate struggle to maintain the Idea against the powers of Chaos without and the unconscious muttering deep-down within. . . . The aim once attained —the idea, the entire content of inner possibilities, fulfiled and made externally actual—the Culture suddenly hardens, it mortifies, its blood congeals, its force breaks down, and it becomes Civilization.[1]

The General Electric Corporation came into being as a result of Thomas A. Edison's fertile mind. He spent virtually all his time in his laboratory, and it was time well spent. He received patents for 1,093 inventions and created the phonograph, the electric locomotive, motion pictures, the mimeograph, and the electric light bulb.

But Edison was no business genius. He had a terrible record of business judgment and was constantly in financial difficulty. Edison General Electric was formed in 1889 with the assistance of Henry Villard because Edison had run out of funds to finance his research laboratory.

Would Thomas A. Edison survive in the modern General Electric company? Edison's biographer wrote:

> Rebellion was one of his most notable early characteristics—rebellion against his disciplinarian mother, against a stern and unforgiving church, against a dull and rigid school. From boyhood to old age, he could not bear to have anyone tell him what to do, but remained undisciplined and iconoclastic . . . he was a bright and lonely misfit, who in today's society would have been probed and tested, then pushed, pulled, kneaded, and reshaped to make him conform to "the norm."[2]

They used to say that you could find Edison in his laboratory by following the trail of tobacco juice that he squirted onto the floor. When his wife asked him why he refused to use a spittoon, he answered that a spittoon was hard to hit, but the floor was difficult to miss. Not only did he have bad habits, but he was an all-around bad manager and poor communicator. The modern General Electric would likely have had very little to do with Thomas Edison.

When it comes to inventors, Edison is not unique. He lived in the world of ideas, ideas that he brought to tangible fruition and practical application, but only with the help of more practical personalities. "My business is thinking," Edison proclaimed. "The man who doesn't make up his mind to cultivate the habit of thinking misses the greatest pleasures in life."

Thomas Edison, Henry Ford, Stephen Wozniak, An Wang, and tens of thousands of lesser-known founders and inventors were all Prophets who generated the basic idea, the creative impulse that powered the eventual result—the entity we call the corporation.

THE CHARACTER OF THE PROPHET

To understand the Prophet, we must appreciate the power of ideas and the spirit often associated with those ideas. Ideas are the seed of material creation. Ideas are the foundation of great corporations. Ideas are what power all social and religious revolutions. And in promoting their ideas over the established order, Prophets are technological—or social—revolutionaries.

> *The Revolution was effected before the war commenced. The Revolution was in the minds and hearts of the people; a change in their religious sentiments, their duties and obligations. This radical change in the principles, opinions, sentiments and affections of the people was the real American Revolution.*
>
> —JOHN ADAMS, 1818

Great men of ideas possess personalities that set them apart from the crowd. Just as their ideas and inventions do not conform to the status quo, neither, as a rule, will their behavior. It is arguable whether Prophets succeed despite their personalities, or because their personalities contribute to the generation of ideas.

Consider Isaac Newton. Born on Christmas Day 1642, Newton entered an English family of absolutely no distinction. The pains inflicted during childhood easily explain his adult eccentricities but give no clue to his genius.

His father, a farmer who could not sign his name, died three months before Newton's birth. He soon lost his mother as well. Within two years she married a wealthy minister who insisted that Isaac be reared by his grandmother while she raised the minister's children. For nine years, until his stepfather's death, he was separated from his mother, and Isaac remembered "threatening my father and mother to burn them and the house over them." Psychotic episodes during his adult life can be traced to the trauma of his childhood.

As with many who live in the world of ideas, Newton was inept at handling practical affairs. When his stepfather died, Newton's mother inherited his property and decided that her firstborn son should manage it. However, Isaac, now immersed in books, botched the job. At school he was not known as a brilliant student but was remembered for building mechanical models, clocks, and windmills. He was already toying with the laws of physics and mathematics.

Newton enrolled in Trinity College, Cambridge, in June of 1661. When he received his bachelor's degree four years later, the most profound undergraduate career had ended. With virtually no guidance, Newton had created a new philosophy and a new form of mathematics. But he had confined his writings to his own notebooks.

The anonymity did not last long. Within two years Newton had become the most important scientist alive. His *Principia (The Mathematical Principles of Natural Philosophy)* is considered the most important scientific book ever written. It defines the laws of motion and of universal gravitation. Newton explained the movements of the earth, the moon, and the planets; he explained the tides and precise shape of the earth. And he wrote it in just eighteen months. Newton wrote mathematics the way Mozart wrote symphonies—it appeared to come naturally.

Later Newton would move to London, become attracted to the excitement of the city, and eventually be appointed warden and master of the mint. It is important to note that once Sir Isaac became involved in the worldly affairs of London, his creative and scientific contributions ceased. He seems to have traded creativity for practicality.

But for all his success, Newton was not happy. Historian Richard Westfall, who devoted twenty years to writing Newton's biography, called him "a tortured man, an extremely neurotic personality who teetered always, at least through middle age, on the verge of breakdown." A colleague called Newton's "the most fearful, cautious, and suspicious temper that I ever knew." Among his few personal friends, none of whom were women, were John Locke and Samuel Pepys. During one of his psychotic fits he turned on both men, accusing them of conspiracies, and refused to see them again.

Newton made few apologies for his eccentricities. Like Thomas Edison and Henry Ford, he was obsessed by his work. John Maynard Keynes, the economist and Newton scholar, claimed that "Newton was capable of greater sustained mental effort than any man before or since." Once he began on a problem, he worked relentlessly, forgetting to eat or sleep. Shortly before his death, Newton wrote this description of his life:

> I don't know what I may seem to the world. But, as to myself, I seem to have been only like a boy playing on the seashore and diverting myself in now and then finding a smoother pebble or prettier shell than ordinary, whilst the great ocean of truth lay undiscovered before me.

It is a surprise to some that this Prophet of science, who wrote the most brilliant mathematical dissertation the world had ever seen, also devoted more than a decade to interpreting the Bible, particularly the Book of Revelations. But as we come to understand Prophets, there is little surprise. They are explorers of ideas, all ideas.

This pursuit provides their motivation. Just as the average youngster learns to enjoy the manipulation of blocks and balls, the creative genius, perhaps forced by painful experience or the denial of more common pleasures, learns instead the pleasures that can be contained within the mind. There are other differences as well. The average youth graduates from playing with blocks and balls to the orderly process of conforming to assignments, completing tasks, and following the prescriptions of superiors. However, the creative personality appears to take a detour, failing to conform to the order of others and, instead, shifting his field to an internal play of ideas.

While some businesses are often founded with the singular intent of making money, these firms rarely make significant contributions to the marketplace because they present no new creation. The founder who creates a new product or service in response to a recognized challenge contributes to the wealth of society. This is the difference between our Prophet and the founder of a common business. The Prophet, whether he is found in business or elsewhere, is rarely motivated by the desire for material comfort and pleasure. He is motivated by ideas.

In their book, *Breakthroughs!*, P. R. Nayak and J. M. Ketteringham report how product innovations actually occur. Their research exposes a number of myths about product innovation:

Myth: Big success requires big resources.

Reality: The sort of people who devise and drive breakthrough ideas are almost never motivated by the prospect of making money. Rather, they are obsessed with solving a problem.

Myth: Breakthroughs always respond to an unfulfilled need in the marketplace.

Reality: In every case, it was clear that the spark was the curiosity of an individual. Often the originator intended eventually to sell some sort of product. But, again, neither profit potential nor market intelligence

played a significant role in any of the breakthrough begin-
nings we studied.[3]

The creative personality is likely to conflict with the mature
culture or corporation. It is easy to see why.

In maturity the corporation is dominated by material reality—
producing goods consistently, reliably, predictably. The more ec-
centric the creative personality, the more unpredictable, and so the
greater the likelihood of conflict. Not surprisingly, then, corporate
managers are likely to send their Prophets into exile. Prophets
represent a violation of corporate values. They don't respect rigid
and venerable institutions. They value ideas—ideas that often include the inevitable collapse of the old order.

The persecution of Prophets is a story as old as history. They
are banished to wander in the wilderness, desert, or mountains.
There they are free to focus their energies until their ideas burn to
be revealed.

Compassion dictates that banishment and isolation are wicked
and unjust punishments. However, it may be that some kind of
persecution is the necessary challenge, the hardship, that galvanizes
human character to the point where it is strong enough to forge an
entirely new creation.

You May Be a Prophet If . . .

. . . your ideas are long-range and visionary.

. . . you are willing to make great sacrifices in time and energy
to see your ideas realized.

. . . you tend to withdraw for long periods to work through
your ideas.

. . . others see you as a bit "different."

. . . you're probably not very well organized, and you are im-
patient with details.

PROPHETS IN HISTORY

History demonstrates that the development of civilization is achieved in response to challenges. A culture that achieves a state of satisfaction reaches a static condition. Progress ends. A society that is dissatisfied enters into a period of change; it progresses when it is in motion.

And that motion is often disquieting. Civilizations have been forged out of the most difficult physical, social, economic, and spiritual conditions, from the jungles of Central America to the sands of the Egyptian desert. British historian Arnold Toynbee concluded: "We have ascertained that civilizations come to birth in environments that are unusually difficult and not unusually easy," and he confirms the social law that "the greater the challenge, the greater the stimulus" to growth.[4]

It is ironic that both companies and people seek comfort and certainty, when those very conditions are the ones most likely to bring about decline. The muscles of the body must be challenged in order to develop or maintain optimal condition. The human mind requires the same exercise to develop and prevent degeneration and senility. And the law of challenge and response applies equally to all organizations. No society, or business, ever developed significantly in the absence of challenges.

It is the Prophet who responds to challenge and who provides the challenge to the established order. We know the Prophets' names because of their undeniable impact, regardless of their Divinity. Moses, Jesus, Mohammed, Buddha, and Krishna all raised the phoenix of new vision and direction out of the ashes of an old and corrupt society. They all generated the impetus necessary for the building of a new culture, through their manner, utterance, and personality.

All were dedicated to their world of ideas and were willing to abandon the world of material form. All confronted the established authority. And all were accused of troublemaking or heresy and were rejected, if not exiled or crucified.

None was particularly good at administering. Indeed, they never really tried to translate their beliefs into an organized religion.

Buddha, for example, devoted much of his life to meditation and self-imposed starvation while he pursued his Eight-Fold Path. If it had been left to the singular talents of the Prophets, there would have been no Buddhist, Islamic, Hindu, or Christian civilizations. Yet without them, the world would have remained in the darkness of decay.

The great religions and their Prophets are the force that has most repeatedly, through history, stimulated a renewal of the individual character and the collective conscience. They have always appeared during a period of desolation, a period of extreme need, of extreme challenge, requiring a revolutionary response. The Arabian desert of the seventh century presented conditions as challenging as those faced by any previous Prophet.

Mohammed was born to the poverty of Arabia in A.D. 570. His birthplace of Mecca was a city of 20,000 to 25,000 people and was a place of pilgrimage. The Kaaba was the focus of the pilgrimage, a small square temple containing a meteorite, which was regarded as a god and looked over all of the little tribal gods. In nearby towns there were Jewish and Christian settlements, but there was no unifying religion or dominant philosophy that brought the tribes together. Indeed, they worshiped hundreds of tribal gods. The tribes, engaged in constant treachery, battled and pillaged mercilessly. There were no standards of cleanliness, hygiene, or even privacy; people walked into one another's homes unannounced, even when a man was closeted with his wife.

Yet Mohammed was able to unify these people. At first blush, he was an unlikely savior. He lived the life of a merchant until he was forty. It is doubtful that he ever learned to write. The source of his inspiration is the pivotal religious question. Historians who are Christian or secularists will argue that he learned many of his ideas from the Jewish and Christian communities. Islamic writers adhere to Mohammed's own explanation that the angel Gabriel appeared to him on Mount Hirra and delivered the redeeming message.

The story goes that Gabriel held up a tablet for Mohammed to read, but he could not read. Again, Gabriel commanded him to read, and he protested that he could not. A third time he was commanded, and then the revelation reached him: "Read in the Name of the Lord

Who created; Who created Man of blood congealed. Read, the Lord is the Most Beneficent; Who taught by the Pen; Who teacheth Man what he knoweth not." Then in the stillness of the lone hillside, the clear voice rang out again, to tell Mohammed that God had chosen Him to be His Messenger to mankind.

Mohammed went to his followers and asked them to renounce the worship of their many tribal gods and to accept the reality of the One True God. It was not a simple request. He was asking his followers to divorce themselves from the entire social milieu of Meccan society, to become social revolutionaries. But this is the pattern with all Prophets. They do not ask simply for the acceptance of an intellectual idea, but for a change in social identity.

Yet Mohammed succeeded. His influence can be measured by the power the Islamic world achieved in the following six hundred to eight hundred years. The Islamic cities such as Cordoba in Spain and Adrianople in Turkey stood as clear testimony to the progress brought by Mohammed's revelation. When the Muslims drove out the Visigoths from Spain, they rebuilt the destroyed Cordoba and made the city of one million people the largest and most cultured in Europe, famous for its art, architecture, industry, and scholarship. The principal library alone contained over four hundred thousand volumes. The streets were paved, the courts of justice adhered to written law. Civil administration was orderly.

In stark contrast, Paris and London at this time were centers of ignorance and superstition, dominated by feudal war lords, lacking any formal administration or system of justice, the streets covered with mud and the population infested with disease.

The current conduct of some of his followers notwithstanding, Mohammed taught tolerance for people of all faiths and a strong sense of the need for justice, education, and social order. And because it was exactly the message that met the needs of his fellow men, they responded. Their belief became so strong that they decided to enlighten the rest of the world. Unification, inspiration, mobilization, these are the consequences of the Prophetic act.

There is a pattern in the life of Prophets. Their creative impulse at some point forces them to withdraw from society. Jesus went to the desert and Mohammed to the mountains. Buddha, Krishna, and Confucius all went through periods of withdrawal from society where they nurtured their inspiration before re-emerging as catalysts for social change.

Lesser Prophets have also gone through this cycle of withdrawal and return. Saint Benedict was born to a traditional upper-class family and educated in Rome. Later he withdrew into the wilderness to live in a cave for three years. Saint Gregory was born and bred in Rome and became a career bureaucrat before he gave up all his secular positions and wealth and withdrew—again for three years—to a monastic life. Similarly, Lenin, Machiavelli, Kant, and Dante, among others, withdrew from society and eventually returned to preach their gospel. Withdrawal appears to be a requirement, so that the Prophet can not only form his ideas, but also gather his powers and focus the spiritual strength that will lead and change a culture.

PROPHETS IN BUSINESS

We did no market research, we had no sales forecasts, no return-on-investment calculations. None of that. I very simply built my dream car and figured that there would be other people who share that dream.

—Dr. Porsche

To my knowledge, no business Prophet has ever claimed his creation was the result of divine inspiration. Prophets of business, like those of science, respond to the challenges of their environment. They often developed their vision while working as salesmen, listening to their customers, and recognizing a new customer need. They may have developed their vision while working in production, tinkering with new applications of old materials, thus inventing a new product. They may have had all of the normal personality characteristics of sales or production managers, but now, having found what they believe to be their true mission, their personality takes on new form.

The creation of McDonald's is the story of several complex personalities, each fulfilling a vital role. Ray Kroc is often mistakenly called the founder of McDonald's, but the creation was not his. He was an entrepreneur, yes, but of a different stripe. He was the Barbarian locked in a combatlike struggle to conquer the territory.

Richard and Maurice (Mac) McDonald of San Bernardino were the Prophets. They opened their first drive-in restaurant just east of Pasadena in 1937. In California the car had already come to dominate the landscape—both physically and culturally—and the brothers met with success. So did Bob Wian, whose Glendale drive-in became Bob's, Home of the Big Boy. The McDonald brothers' success led, in 1940, to a second and larger restaurant, which became the town's number-one teenage hangout. The menu offered twenty-five items, and twenty carhops served as many as 125 cars crowded into the lot. Soon the McDonalds were splitting $50,000 a year in profits, considerable wealth in those days. But they quickly became bored. They needed a new challenge.

Mac and Dick began to examine the elements of their business. They noted that 80 percent of sales came from hamburgers. They also saw that the more they attracted the teenaged crowd, the less they saw of families and older people. They also found the young carhops to be unreliable employees. Then the brothers made a decision that few successful businessmen would dare to make. They would close down their successful drive-in and completely revamp its format.

Taking such a risk is entirely consistent with the character of the Prophet. However, its successful outcome required the meticulous pursuit of efficiency that is found in the Builder. The McDonald brothers were capable of handling both roles. They decided to reshape their business and focus on speed of service and keeping costs low.

Dick McDonald put it this way:

> Our whole concept was based on speed, lower prices, and volume. We were going after big, big volumes by lowering prices and by having the customer serve him-

self. My God, the carhops were slow. We'd say to ourselves that there had to be a faster way.

The cars were jamming up the lot. Customers weren't demanding it, but our intuition told us that they would like speed. Everything was moving faster. The supermarkets and dime stores had already converted to self-service, and it was obvious the future of drive-ins was self-service. [5]

When the McDonalds opened their redesigned drive-in, they had replaced its one 3-foot-long grill with two 6-foot grills they designed and built themselves. They invented other equipment, too, including a stainless-steel lazy Susan that held twenty-four hamburger buns to be "dressed" by two crewmen. Paper bags, wrappers, and cups replaced china and flatware. The twenty-five menu items were cut to nine, and all hamburgers were topped the same: ketchup, mustard, onions, and two pickles. Thus hamburgers could be prepared ahead of demand. Like Henry Ford, the McDonalds opted for mass production and lower prices. The new price of their hamburgers? Fifteen cents.

The new McDonald's Restaurant was a hit. The cars of southern California were soon in line, twenty deep during peak hours, and the drive-in was producing sales 40 percent above the preconversion rate. The brothers had achieved the increased sales, *decreasing* both their capital investment and labor costs by a third.

The McDonald brothers had risen to the challenge presented by the automobile, the fast-paced California life-style, and the deficiencies of the common carhop drive-ins. Innovation—successful innovation—was their response.

Such success was anything but a secret. In July 1952, *American Restaurant Magazine* ran a cover story on McDonald's, and the brothers were bombarded with requests for information.

"So many people were coming to see us that Mac and I were spending most of our time just talking to them. We knew then we had to have a franchise agent," Dick McDonald recalled.

Dick and Mac did make some effort to capitalize on their success through franchising, but they didn't have the same passion for expansion that they had for invention. And perhaps it is here that the Prophet must change his style and motivations or be replaced by a new character. The McDonalds were now content. And perhaps a bit conservative. When Neil Fox of Phoenix applied for the first franchise, he wanted to call it McDonald's. Dick McDonald snorted, "What the hell for? McDonald's means nothing in Phoenix!"

Progress depends on an energetic and creative response to new challenges. It can stop when a condition of ease is reached. "We couldn't spend all the money we were making," the brothers said. "We were taking it easier and having a lot of fun doing what we wanted to do." Dick and Mac had achieved a condition of ease.

The business press has exalted the entrepreneur, as well it should. Any catalog of the heroes of enterprise should include those who invent, rise, and succeed. These brothers could be described in business terms as entrepreneurs. However, the term "entrepreneur" lumps together two very different functions, the originator of the idea and the commander who takes the idea and runs with it. The Prophet may have both qualities, or he may only have one.

McDonald's evolution and continuing success now required a new kind of leader, the Barbarian, who could perceive the current challenges and rise to meet them. Ray Kroc was his name, and expanding territory was his game. The rest, as they say, is history.

Creating the vision and energy upon which an enterprise is built is like a chemical reaction. Sometimes that creation is the work of one individual, as in the case of Henry Ford. It may be the work of a small team. Or it may be, as in the case of Schlumberger, the work of a family.

In November of 1919, a father and two sons founded Schlumberger, today one of the leading suppliers of petroleum technology. Paul Schlumberger, the father, had been in the textile machinery business. He was a visionary who loved science and engineering. He invested in projects like the Suez Canal, a pinnacle of scientific and engineering achievement at the time. Son Conrad's great passion was science. He taught physics in Paris while doing original experiments using electricity to measure the earth's subsurface. Paul's other son, Marcel, studied civil engineering. More practical and more cautious than his brother, Marcel Schlumberger developed into a shrewd businessman.

Paul Schlumberger was impressed with Conrad's scientific work. He gave up his own business, moved to Paris, and convinced Marcel to join them in a partnership to develop the technology Conrad was exploring. Paul wrote an agreement that he and his two sons signed. It reveals much about the motivations and priorities of the three men and influenced the culture of the company for many years to come.

> For their part my sons agree not to dilute their efforts by working in other areas. . . . In this undertaking, the interests of scientific research take precedence over financial ones. I will be kept informed of, and may give my opinion on, important developments and the necessary expenses required. The money given by me is my contribution to a work primarily scientific and secondarily practical. . . . Marcel will bring to Conrad his remarkable ability as an engineer and his common sense. Conrad, on the other hand, will be the man of science. I will support them.[6]

The contract between Paul Schlumberger and his sons is eloquent in its simplicity and clear priorities. If you want to create a successful company, first create an excellent product.

The brothers pursued their scientific research until 1927, when they received their first contract from a petroleum exploration company to use their technology in exploration. From then until now, Schlumberger has dominated oil field technology. Its net worth is now almost $20 billion, and it still maintains its reputation for scientific excellence.

Business Prophets, like those of science, tend to be nonconformists. Several years ago I conducted a study for the Honeywell Corporation during which I visited all their recent acquisitions and interviewed their chief executives. In a number of cases, the CEOs of the acquired companies were the Prophet founders. I will never forget the president of one high-tech company. He was the "genius" engineer who had developed the product and given birth to the firm. His office was in unbelievable disarray. Piles of papers and files lay everywhere; publications on the floor beyond count. (His desk looked like the floor of my seven-year-old's bedroom after a week of parental inattention.) The president's personal appearance matched that of his office.

I could understand the confusion of the founder's office. What surprised me was that Honeywell not only tolerated it, but condoned it. There was no pressure on him to conform to the otherwise clean and orderly norms of the Honeywell Corporation. The terms of the acquisition of his company included the understanding that he would continue to provide the technical guidance to the firm, and that traditional "Honeywellers" would handle the administrative tasks for which he had little talent or interest. It was the right way to manage a Prophet.

The creative act of leadership is the act of unreasonable men and women. God save us from the corporation that insists that these people conform.

HOW TO GET ALONG WITH A PROPHET

If You Work for a Prophet . . .

. . . don't expect him to provide specific objectives or instructions. He is more likely to send you out on vague missions. Ask him to discuss your objectives, then write your own based on your discussion and provide him with a copy.

. . . don't expect him to follow up on the details of your work. He doesn't care. Talk to him about the larger goals toward which you are working and how those goals fit into his vision.

. . . seek out the Prophet for advice and his ideas, particularly on large and visionary issues. Every Prophet values thinking and believes that others who enjoy discussing ideas are also among the wise.

. . . be tolerant of his latest idea. It may sound crazy, impractical, and a complete change in direction. Don't confront him with all that is wrong with his brainstorm. He is sensitive and doesn't want to have his ideas squelched. Ask him leading questions that will help him evaluate his own ideas. How will it fit into the larger company plan? He shares his ideas with you so that you will help him think them through to a practical decision. He will value you if you help him shape his brainstorm into practical courses of action.

. . . do not feel that you need to compete on the Prophet's field of play. He doesn't expect others to have his same characteristics. Prophets tend to clash with other Prophets. He desires complementary characteristics. He appreciates the person of action who gets things accomplished and the administrator who gets things organized, as long as they don't insist that he be organized.

If a Prophet Works for You . . .

. . . you are lucky! Recognize him for his creative abilities, reinforce and encourage those talents. Do not demand that he be well organized or conform to standard procedures.

. . . he needs you to listen. He needs to know that his visionary ideas are important to you. Let him know that within your company there is room and opportunity for the implementation of his ideas.

. . . help him distinguish between his "regular" job and his creative activities. He may need to justify his salary with mundane work.

. . . protect him from the Bureaucrats. Remember that in mature companies Prophets are all too often crucified.

. . . have patience. Prophets work not for this quarter's results, but for the impact they can have over the long run. Their view is very long range. Insistence on immediate results destroys creativity.

THE PROPHET ORGANIZATION

The new company can hardly be recognized as an organization. The prophet may have little more than inspiration and dedication to his ideas. He may have a name for his product and firm but little capital and few (if any) employees or customers. An outsider looking at this young organism would undoubtedly be shocked by its lack of conformity to standard business practices. There may be no accounting, few if any records, no legal documents.

It is a period dominated by personality, not policies and procedures. And the personality of the leader is not likely to instill stability. The Prophet can drive his employees crazy with his radical, and often unexplained, changes in course. He may decide over the weekend to reorganize and announce the new organization Monday morning without consulting anyone else. Traditional systems of management, like appraisal, review, promotion, vacation policy, and so on, may not even exist.

It is important to understand that in the first stage of a culture this is not only normal, but desirable. Prophets can succeed only when they have the flexibility to move quickly without regard to administrative procedures. Those working in a newborn company must be prepared to do anything and everything that needs to be done. Forget about formal decision making, chains of command, and the like. There won't be any.

Prophets do not usually make effective consensus decision makers. They believe too strongly in their own ideas. They may listen to the ideas of others, but it is difficult for them to give other people's ideas equal merit. They have fought for their own beliefs, and if they have succeeded in founding their own company, they have been rewarded for sticking to their ideas. As long as those ideas work, the Prophet's determination is an advantage. Once he strays from his area of expertise, he is in trouble.

The business Prophet is likely to inspire a small group of highly dedicated and loyal followers. Those followers will describe their "guru" in glowing terms. He is the genius whose concept created the business. He often seems above the plane of other mortals. There is a dangerous halo effect that surrounds the Prophet. His followers are reluctant to give him negative feedback. He may go unquestioned in his judgment, even when he is making decisions in areas in which he has no more than ordinary knowledge. Herein lies a great danger, one that has been the downfall of many company founders.

In the organization dominated by a Prophet, there is likely to be a very strong sense of mission. The early days of Apple Computer, and other recent high-tech firms, well illustrate the excitement of the Age of the Prophet. The Prophet's apostles will work sixteen-hour days and sacrifice much. They aren't just working at a job. They honestly believe that they have a once-in-a-lifetime opportunity to "make a statement."

But is the Prophet the only one who can spur innovation? Can't management treat the process of innovation in a systematic manner the way it handles other activities? Peter Drucker argues that innovation is

> capable of being presented as a discipline, capable of being learned, capable of being practiced. Entrepreneurs need to search purposefully for the sources of innovation, the changes and their symptoms that indicate opportunities for successful innovation.[7]

Drucker is right. Particularly within mature companies, the process of innovation can be stimulated, encouraged, and rewarded. Throughout the established company, these employees who exhibit the visionary qualities of the Prophet must be drawn out by management. To pave the way for innovation, we must create systems that open channels for ideas and energy that might otherwise be blocked. A system that provides an ongoing forum where engineers or chemists or architects can discuss advances and applications of their technology stimulates creativity.

Social and monetary rewards for employees who propose new product applications will not only set a precedent, but spur new ideas. Systematic training of managers in team leadership skills will enable managers and employees to engage in a free flow of ideas. Systems must be enabling systems, rather than systems that control.

From the research organizations of Bell Labs, IBM, and the large pharmaceutical companies have come thousands of innovations that have not only dramatically enhanced their companies' progress, but changed our world. Within these companies, creative people are not only tolerated, but encouraged. Johnson & Johnson and 3M have done a particularly good job of fostering internal entrepreneurship and rewarding people who develop new products. Such farsighted practices permit Prophets to survive in the mature corporation.

Your Organization Is in the Prophetic Age If . . .

. . . your leader is a visionary and creative person on whose ideas the company was founded.

. . . your organization is at risk because it has not yet proved its product's viability in the marketplace.

. . . things seem chaotic, changing almost daily.

. . . there is an excitement and deep belief in what you are trying to accomplish.

CHALLENGES AND TASKS

The Response to Personal Crisis Pete Petit's son was six months old when he was found dead in his crib. Sudden Infant Death Syndrome, or "crib death," strikes without warning. There is no cry, whimper, or cough. No hint of trouble. No chance for a father to make any effort to save his child.

Following his son's death, there were sleepless nights and the psychological and social withdrawal that follows personal tragedy. There was also irrational guilt and self-blame.

But within Pete Petit there was also the ability to respond to this tragedy. For the next several months, Pete, an engineer at Lockheed-Georgia, read everything ever written on SIDS. He consulted pediatricians and other experts. It was all disappointing. Finally he realized that if the child's breathing and pulse were monitored electronically, any interruption could be detected. An alarm could sound to warn the parents. If his son had had such a device, Pete was certain he could have saved him.

For months Pete was obsessed with building such a device. He increasingly withdrew from social contacts and devoted less energy to his work at Lockheed. Finally, after several years of research, he developed an electronic infant monitor that became an accepted standard in identifying SIDS risk. He formed a company, Healthdyne, Inc., to develop and market this and other products. Soon Healthdyne grew to a $100 million company.

Pete Petit did not plan to become an entrepreneur. It was the challenge of personal crisis that elicited his creative response.

Flight from Oppressive Bureaucracy Bureaucracy is the institutionalized structure, systems, and behavior that attempts to effect conformity. By definition, bureaucracy is oppressive and a challenge to the creative individual. The creative individual cannot "do his own thing" under the pressure of bureaucracy. And bureaucracy, because of its inherent inability to respond, cannot create an environment that would allow him to. Too often the truly creative individual must rebel or flee the bureaucratic environment.

Much of the world today is dominated by bureaucracies. It is no secret our federal government qualifies. So do many of our large and decaying corporations. However, these bureaucracies are minor compared with the massive structures of oppression that dominate the communist world. If you are a creative individual living in the Ukraine, your opportunities for creative expression may be nonexistent.

Curiously enough, the bureaucratic society ninety miles off the coast of Florida has proved a veritable seedbed of creative individuals for the United States. By stifling enterprise within Cuba, Castro has stimulated a creative explosion in Dade County, Florida, which has become the receiving ground for Cuban immigrants. Today, among the Cuban immigrants you will find more than two hundred new millionaires. Says Chamber of Commerce leader Lester Freeman: "The best thing that's happened to Miami since air-conditioning was when Fidel Castro read Karl Marx."[8]

Thanks to these immigrants, Dade County—now 40 percent Cuban—has maintained one of the lowest rates of unemployment in the country and the lowest unemployment rate in Florida. Florida is second only to California in job creation. Texas is third, making the three states with the highest rates of immigration also the three with the highest rates of job creation.

Too many Americans have not yet learned the lesson of the immigrant. Every wave of immigration is met with cries of "There goes the neighborhood!" The facts are that each fresh influx has brought a new wave of creative and enterprising energy, the very spirit that is most "American." Indeed, the newest to our shores often best reflects the most admired qualities of the American character.

Rebelling Against Unjust Rewards Just as immigrants flee their countries in pursuit of their just rewards, thousands of talented and creative people flee their corporations in the same pursuit. The founders of many new corporations performed successfully within their established firms. Their superiors probably judged them well challenged and rewarded. Yet the Prophet is one dominated by his own mind and spirit, not the estimate of others. If he feels frustrated by bureaucratic blocks, he is likely to strike off on his own path. Often the large, mature corporation is father to dozens of offspring. These infant businesses are headed by discontented and creative individuals who saw that they could not receive in the mature company the recognition, promotion, money, or responsibility their performance merited. Ironically, many of them owe their success to bosses who failed to listen. If their employers had been receptive to their new ideas, many millionaire entrepreneurs might be working away happily within the confines of large corporations.

The Call of New Technology There are dozens of examples of the challenges created by new technology producing creative responses. How many engineers have gone home at night puzzled by a technological problem and, in their bath or bed, created a solution that is now a product on the market? How many men and women, dreaming about what could be done with application of a new technology, went on to form their own company to exploit the opportunity?

As technology advances, we see more and more new entrepreneurial Prophets rising in response. Often they come from unlikely places. Witness the progenitors of Apple Computer, Steven Jobs and Stephen Wozniak. Or William Gates, father of MS-DOS and founder of Microsoft, Inc., the leading microcomputer software company.

It happens that in each of these cases the Prophets were young people who at first were literally playing with the new technologies. Indeed, many of our current crop of creative corporate founders are young, still in their own period of instability, rapid growth, personal exploration, and natural creativity. But whatever their ages, Prophets seem to share the same characteristics and sure response to challenge.

From Creative Mania to Management The creative spark sets its fire and must pass on. Business Prophets are the center of activity during the initial creative stage when the ideas and vision are taking shape. But once the company is ongoing, the Prophet must either take on a completely new role—that of manager—or step aside. Either of these alternatives is immensely difficult.

Recently I consulted with one entrepreneur who had developed his product and was highly successful in managing the company during its early stage. He was successful because he did everything. He worked eighteen-hour days and virtually held the hands of the production workers. Obviously this could not last as the company grew. As he began to delegate, he always had the feeling—and conveyed it to his subordinates—that if he were managing everything himself, it would be going more smoothly. His subordinates constantly felt his lack of approval. He also failed to respect their decisions, violating the chain of command by giving direction to workers and managers several levels down in the organization. Turnover among his managers was extremely high. Eventually this Prophet entrepreneur was booted out by his own board of directors.

It is not uncommon for the Prophet to transcend his first role and develop the qualities of Barbarian. It is, however, fairly uncommon for an individual to transcend more than one period, and it is rare—and extremely heroic—to transcend more than two life cycle phases.

In 1969 Milton G. Kuolt II founded Thousand Trails, Inc., to provide time-sharing campgrounds for recreational vehicle owners. It was Kuolt's first entrepreneurial venture, and he hit it big. Thousand Trails had 27,600 members who paid average membership prices of $5,795 to share a parcel of land in one of the Thousand Trails preserves. The company began with Kuolt and his kids chopping down the underbrush at his campsites and grew into a company with over nine hundred employees and annual sales of $40 million. But Kuolt became increasingly uncomfortable with the success of his company. " 'I don't like this, I can't get my hand around this anymore,' he used to say." [9] Recognizing his own enjoyment in creating the idea and getting it started, and his dislike for the routine of management, Kuolt brought in a chairman and CEO and sold most of his stock.

Not one to sit on his millions, Kuolt next started an airline, Horizon Air Industries, based in Seattle and serving the Pacific Northwest. Again Kuolt was successful. Within a relatively few years, Horizon saw revenues of about $50 million and served twenty destinations with thirty planes.

When Kuolt's first enterprise matured, he got out. With the second one, he wanted to hang on. "I drive my people. You've got to understand that. I work them hard, unmercifully." And as Horizon Air grew, the conflict grew. Each small problem Kuolt found—cold coffee, passengers waiting in line too long—he attacked directly. Yet the systems, the flow of information and scheduling, for example, which were now the important matters, were not being properly addressed. His managers tried to have planning meetings without him. He concluded—and rightly so—that they were revolting against his leadership.

"His style was completely appropriate for the first two or three years, but now we need a different style, a more traditional organizational style of managing a going concern," said one of his managers. "We're no longer flailing around and growing and trying to find ourselves. We're a major company that needs to be managed."

The *Inc.* magazine reporter who interviewed Kuolt noted, "It made me sad to watch him—a kind of faltering hero figure, his usual blustering bravado now broken in places by moments of quiet self-doubt." If Milt Kuolt, multimillionaire, entrepreneurial hero, Prophet/Barbarian, proves unable to change his management style, we can write the conclusion. The company will lose good people; service will decline; costs will suddenly rise ahead of revenues.

The Prophet who founds a company has succeeded by following his own ideas and instincts. He did not accomplish his creation by delegating the task to others. The creator is possessed with the most intense form of personal accountability for his creation. A desirable trait for a creator, it can be the cause of failure in a manager.

◆

The Barbarian

Crisis and Conquest

Every successful enterprise requires three men—a dreamer, a businessman, and a son-of-a-bitch.
—PETER MACARTHUR, 1904

We've seen his smiling, boyish face on television a hundred times. Looking right into the camera, he holds up an electric shaver and says: "I liked it so much, I bought the company." And from all outward appearances you might think Victor Kiam has always gotten by on a smile and a clean shave. Forget it. Kiam is a Barbarian, the term I will use for the person who embraces the Prophet's values and vision, then leads his company on its conquering march. Without the Barbarian, there would be neither civilization nor corporation—and there certainly would be no Remington Shaver Corp. today.

When Sperry sold the company to Kiam, who had had a relatively traditional career with Lever Bros., it wasn't doing him any favors. Sperry got rid of it because it was a loser. Remington shavers were competing in a difficult market and had little prospect for either growth or profit. Suddenly corporate manager Kiam faced a life-or-death struggle that is the necessary environment and natural element of the Barbarian.

Almost immediately Kiam fired more than seventy executives from the relatively small company. Many more fled in fear. To those who remained, Kiam dictated the terms of his conquest as he stood in the middle of the plant floor. "There is no blue collar and white collar. There is only one collar—the Remington collar!"

He eliminated executive washrooms, made medical plans the same for everyone, and quickly created performance incentives for each employee. If this was a matter of life or death for Kiam, he was going to make sure his employees felt the same urgency. He organized them into teams that would have a voice in the running of their company. Now managers would meet weekly with workers to hear complaints—and suggestions.

In short, Victor Kiam revolutionized and revitalized Remington's culture. In addition to coming up with a pretty good marketing campaign that told how he came to buy the company, he minimized the differentiation—both horizontal and vertical—that builds up in a mature company. Instead of having employees thinking about the differences between labor and management, and the differences between employees in different jobs, he got them thinking about what was important: turning out a great shaver.

Kiam did not seek consensus or consult with his managers and employees before he made these changes. He didn't have the time. He went in with club swinging.

Remington is now a success. The bank loans Kiam used to buy the company were paid off nine years ahead of schedule. While many experts had predicted the demise of manufacturing in the United States, Remington now manufactures and exports more electric shavers to Japan than *all* Japanese companies *combined* sell in the United States. And since Kiam bought the company, hundreds of workers have been hired.

Because he was willing to play the role of Barbarian, Victor Kiam succeeded.

The Barbarian will make two appearances in the life cycle of a company—immediately after the birth of the business and again during times of renewal, when the excess baggage of bureaucracy must be shaken loose and swept away. His forte is discipline and quick action.

THE CHARACTER OF THE BARBARIAN

It is ridiculous to call this an industry. This is rat eat rat. Dog eat dog. I'll kill 'em, and I'm going to kill 'em before they kill me. You're talking about the American way of survival of the fittest.
—RAY KROC, BUILDER OF MCDONALD'S EMPIRE, 1973

The personality of the Barbarian is well suited to single-minded, even fierce, dedication to a mission. His actions are based as much on his emotional commitment to his goals as to any rational plan. When he talks about his mission, the adrenaline pumps through his veins and the power of his commitment is evident. Others respond to his force with their own excitement.

He completely accepts the work of his Prophet. The usefulness of the new idea, product, or service, and its potential for success, are clear to him. His true faith provides the urgency and tenacity that lights the way for the young company.

Historically it is not uncommon for Prophets to turn into Barbarians. Mohammed not only provided the Word, he also provided the leadership to organize his people for their conquering march.

While the Prophet is the first leader/visionary, the Barbarian is the first leader/manager. He brings others into the organization; he assigns roles and responsibilities; he directs action toward goals; he rewards—and corrects. His manner is not one we usually associate with contemporary management. This Barbarian is a command decision maker, unlikely to consult others or delegate. We are talking about Genghis Khan or Attila the Hun!

This is the "heroic leader" who, whether through intelligence or intuition, understands that the external impression presented to his followers is as important as any decision he makes. He knows both his followers and adversaries will study his every move, and those moves will be theatrically orchestrated for their effect. And if he has any doubts about the battle plan, they will never show. Historian John Keegan said it well:

> Heroic leadership—and leadership—is like priesthood, statesmanship, even genius, a matter of externals almost as much as internalities. The leader of men in warfare can show himself to his followers only through a mask, a mask that he must make for himself, but a mask made in such form as will mark him to men of his time and place as the leader they want and need.[1]

The Barbarian is the leader in the age of warfare, whether on the field of battle or business.

Corporations may find themselves in a desperate fight for survival during their early years and again after they have been lulled to sleep by their size and success and set upon by a more aggressive challenger. The best turnaround artist, the executive most able to reinvigorate a deteriorating culture, is the Barbarian. Lee Iacocca is a Barbarian.

Chrysler Corporation was a bogged-down bureaucracy, lacking vision or the ability to act decisively. It was also an organization quickly running out of cash and time. The Prophets were long gone.

Then Lee Iacocca took charge. In his autobiography, Iacocca reports:

> All through the company, people were scared and despondent. Nobody was doing anything right. I had never seen anything like it. . . . Over a three-year period I had to fire 33 out of the 35 vice presidents. That's one a month! There was so much to do and so little time! I had to eliminate 35 little duchies. I had to bring some cohesion and unity into the company. I had to get rid of the

many people who didn't know what they were doing. I had to replace them by finding guys with experience who could move fast. And I had to install a system of financial controls as quickly as possible. These problems were urgent, and their solutions all pointed in the same direction. I needed a good team of experienced people who could work with me in turning this company around before it completely fell apart.[2]

It is people, people with high energy and creativity, who transform organizations from declining feudal bureaucracies to wealth-producing institutions. Barbarians understand people. Their energy and faith in the future energizes the people who work for them. Barbarians neither overanalyze financial details nor spend time laying complex plans. They attack the core of the business: the ability to provide quality service or products at low cost. They barge through the headquarters staff, with its unnecessary layers of management, and ascertain the needs of the people who are the real producers, the first-line employees, the people who look the customer in the eye.

Iacocca talked directly to his core people. He instilled in them a belief in the future and a sense of mission. He focused his own attention, and therefore everyone's, on the business of the business —providing products and service.

> *To be a successful soldier, you must know history. . . . What you must know is how man reacts. Weapons change, but man, who uses them, changes not at all. To win battles, you do not beat weapons—you beat the soul of the enemy man.*
> —GEORGE S. PATTON IV

Our culture places high value on communication and empathy. Certainly these are important—but not in times of war. If we are going to fight a war, I want to follow a general who is one tough son of a bitch. I want someone who is prepared to kick ass and not worry at every turn about how others feel. When it's war, I'd rather follow General Patton than the participative manager.

*The first EDSer to see a snake kills it. At General Motors,
first thing you do is organize a committee on snakes. Then
you bring in a consultant who knows a lot about snakes.
Third thing you do is talk about it for a year.*

—H. Ross Perot

H. Ross Perot is, without a doubt, a Barbarian. When he
worked for IBM as a salesman, he was a problem. He was able to
attain his annual sales goal only weeks into the year. Then he would
try to come up with other things to do—like convincing his bosses
that the company could do more than just sell hardware. It could,
Perot told them repeatedly, also sell data processing systems and
provide the people to run them. But IBM, even if it is—or was—
the greatest company on earth, is not an environment prepared to
make use of the Barbarian in search of action. So Perot, with $1,000
of capital, no business plan, and no experience managing a business,
started Electronic Data Systems.

Barbarians, like Perot, have great faith in the power of the
human will. They do not need to analyze all the numbers and trends
to determine whether something is likely to occur. They believe in
their own ability to make it occur. It is not surprising, then, that in
a few months Perot had eighteen employees who, along with their
boss, were working eighteen-hour days. And finally, it is not surprising that he raised EDS to dominance in its field and then sold it
to General Motors for $2.5 billion. The man is nothing if not consis-
tent.

To accomplish all this, Perot drew on his military background.
He often used to refer to a painting hung in his office, *Homecoming
Marine,* saying, "We used to whip the Japanese right regularly, and
if we ever decide we want to do it again in the car business, we
can."

Perot succeeded, not because of brilliant ingenuity in product
development and not because of his administrative talents. He succeeded because he is a leader in the classic sense—he acts decisively and can get others to follow. (So devoted were EDS
employees that one day they took Perot out to the parking lot,
dressed him in a suit of armor, and put him up on a white horse.)

With EDS's acquisition by GM, the Barbarian Perot became GM's largest shareholder and sat on its board. But H. Ross Perot, true to his character, could no more sit patiently and watch the elephant plod along than Alexander the Great could have sat and politely applauded the speech making of Athenian scholars. As he did at IBM, Perot spoke out frequently. And the results were the same. In due time he was bought out and banished. GM was convinced that this Barbarian could never understand the complexities and sophistication of its systems. Too bad. It is precisely because GM had those complexities and systems that they needed Perot's influence.

You May Be a Barbarian If . . .

. . . your mission is clear and urgent. Survival is the priority.

. . . you are in charge and very comfortable making decisions.

. . . others accuse you of being authoritarian and not consulting them on decisions.

. . . you are very action-oriented and have little patience with planning and administration.

THE BARBARIAN IN HISTORY

In the history books, the term "barbarian" is most closely associated with the hordes that descended upon the Roman Empire during its days of decline and disintegration. Edward Gibbon's *Decline and Fall of the Roman Empire* is the classic chronicle of the most visible slide of civilization. Here can be seen the twin processes of transition from the old to the new. First, the decadence of the rich and dominant forces of society, which leads to self-destruction, and the parallel attack and rise of youthful and energetic barbarians.

By the fifth century A.D., when the Huns attacked the Roman Empire, much of the conquerors' work had been accomplished from within. The larger social purpose that creates unity and strength was lost. Petty family squabbles were now determining who would sit in the seat of Caesar. For generations the Roman Empire had been eating at its own flesh. Romans gathered in arenas to cheer as their fellow men slaughtered animals, each other, and even children, in endless "games." Carcopino describes it:

> What revolts us is the quantity of victims, the bath of animal blood: 5,000 beasts were killed in one day of the Munera with which Titus inaugurated the Coliseum in A.D. 80. . . . We find mention of two minor shows, one of 350 pairs of gladiators, the other of 2,020, while the major event lasted 117 days in which 4,941 pairs of gladiators took part. Pliny the Younger contended that these massacres were essentially calculated to engender courage by showing how the love of glory and the desire to conquer could lodge even in the breasts of criminals and slaves. These are specious excuses. The thousands of Romans who, day after day, from morning until night, could take pleasure in this slaughter and not spare a tear for those whose sacrifice multiplied their stakes, were learning nothing but contempt for human life and dignity.[3]

This decadence invites conquerors. They came in the form of the Huns.

The Huns—who when massed for battle numbered as many as seven hundred thousand and had conquered all of Asia and Eastern Europe—could not have succeeded without powerful leadership. This leader was Attila, nephew of the former leader of the Huns, Rugilas. Immediately upon his appointment, he and his brother arranged to meet with ambassadors of Constantinople. They met on a spacious plain, on horseback, refusing to dismount and arrogantly dictating terms of peace. Edward Gibbon reports that each demand was an insult to the majesty of the empire:

> If a line of separation were drawn between the civilized and the savage climates of the globe; between the inhabitants of cities, who cultivated the earth, and the hunters and shepherds, who dwelt in tents, Attila might aspire to the title of supreme and sole monarch of the barbarians.

> The haughty step and demeanor of the king of the Huns
> expressed the consciousness of his superiority above the
> rest of mankind; and he had a custom of fiercely rolling
> his eyes, as if he wished to enjoy the terror which he
> inspired.[4]

There is no doubt that Attila was savage in his attacks. It was not uncommon for the Huns to massacre entire populations, sell the women into slavery, and enlist all the able-bodied men into their army. They also razed buildings. The barbarian does not require multifloored buildings with individual rooms with various uses occupied by people of differing rank. He prefers the open plain, filled with common horsemen who sit equally and charge in unison. Though Attila came to dominate western Asia and Eastern Europe, his headquarters was always a temporary encampment.

The Legions of the Empire, like the buildings and property they protected, had grown specialized and complex. The layers of management had increased, and the leaders were increasingly detached from the troops, too involved in politics and ritual, attending ceremonies and games, delegating to their specialized and expansive staff organizations. Even the threat of attack from Attila, Gibbon tells us, could not provoke Theodosius "to interrupt his amusement . . . or to appear in person at the head of the Roman legions."[5]

There were few barriers between Attila and *his* troops. They shared pleasure and pain. They were in the field together, united in purpose. There were few layers of management, few specialized staffs, few differences in perks or pay.

Another example of the conquering leader occurred even earlier, in the fourth century B.C. The leader? Alexander the Great. There was never before, and has never been since, any leader of more heroic proportions, of greater influence on our concept of leadership, than Alexander the Great. He is, perhaps, history's best example of a leader who instilled loyalty and a willingness to sacrifice that made his armies unbeatable.

Again, the stage was set for Alexander by a culture consumed with self-indulgence and vanity. By the fifth century B.C., the city-state of Athens had passed its peak. It was devoted to learning and the arts, and its politics were dominated by men like the great orator Demosthenes, who put his talents into the cause of constant criticism rather than constructive action. The Athenians placed an excessive importance on individualism, inward focus, and the exploration of the "self," an emphasis common among the dominant intellectuals of every decaying society. The ability to focus energies on an expansive destiny, to rally human energies with common social purpose, was past.

Alexander represented the perfect contrast. He was, by our definition, a Barbarian. He assumed command as a youth and acted with youthful urgency and energy. When he was seventeen he was left in charge of the Greek province of Macedon, while his father, Philip, left to attack Byzantium. During Philip's absence Alexander defeated the Thracian tribes who attacked his homeland. Three years later Philip was assassinated and Alexander was elected leader by unanimous acclamation of the Macedonian army.

Only twenty, Alexander became the most powerful leader in the Greek world, and he adopted his father's expansive vision of a world embracing the Greek state, uniting all people in a common enterprise. By his thirtieth birthday he had conquered all of the world known to the Greeks, from the Ionian Sea to Phoenicia, Syria, and Persia all the way to northern India.

The image that remains of Alexander is one of an enlightened, sensitive, and courageous youth. However, our view is skewed by our cultural bias. He was one of us. We, in the Western world, are descendants of his legacy. If we had been on the receiving end of his attack, our view would be very different. The blinding determination of the Barbarian allows little tolerance for those who stand in the way of his mission. Only a few years after taking command of the Macedonian troops, Alexander had conquered all of Greece, destroying four cities. At Thebes, Alexander's army razed its buildings and sold thirty thousand inhabitants into slavery. This terrible act would compare today with direct nuclear strike on a city. The defeat of Thebes signaled the collapse of all Greek resistance to the rule of Alexander, who then turned his march eastward to fulfill his father's dream of conquest. The inhabitants of Gaza who put up fierce resistance met the same fate of slavery and slaughter.

In his book *The Mask of Command,* in which he analyzes the personality of the great commanders, historian John Keegan sees in Alexander the "noble savage."

> There is the nobility of self-forgetting in his life—danger forgotten, wounds forgotten, fatigue forgotten. But they were forgotten with the amnesia of savagery, to which all who opposed his will were subject. His dreadful legacy was to ennoble savagery in the name of glory and to leave a model of command that far too many men of ambition sought to act out in the centuries to come.[6]

But Keegan is mistaken. It is not the model of savagery that subsequent leaders sought to emulate. Rather, they hoped to inspire the same kind of loyalty and devotion conferred on Alexander by his followers, earned through his unquestionable deeds of courage and leadership.

Alexander's greatest military challenge was his defeat of King Darius' mighty Persian army, which had attacked and threatened Greece itself. On the plains of Issus, where he was outnumbered by as much as six to one, Alexander led the charge of his cavalry. He was wounded on every limb of his body, and his Companions (the name by which he referred to his cavalry) gained courage from his personal valor. The Greek chronicler Arrian writes:

> Having launched his shock troops into the river [Alexander] returned to the right wing, gave his war yell, and riding into the front, drove straight into the massive formation drawn up on purpose to receive him. He directed his thrust towards the Persian high command, traditionally in the center, rescuing some of his own assault troops who were hard pressed.[7]

Darius retreated. The mighty Persian army broke and ran. The Macedonian troops pursued the Persians for twenty-five miles and slaughtered tens of thousands. After the battle, Alexander visited his wounded warriors, Arrian tells us, "looking at their wounds, asking them how they got them, encouraging each to tell about his deeds and even brag of them." Alexander gave special funeral honors to the twenty-five fallen Companions, granted tax remissions to their families, and had their likenesses cast in bronze. In *The Nature of Alexander,* biographer Mary Renault notes, "Glimpses like this explain the extraordinary relationship that was to evolve between him and his army in the ensuing years."[8]

Leadership in the second stage of evolution is that of deeds, not words. It was Alexander's deeds that created loyalty, not only in his "Companions," but in his conquered subjects as well. Renault gives this insight:

> Without doubt, the love of the army was the breath of life to him; but never in his life did he try to get it cheap. It was not just a matter of being first into danger and last to take comforts when conditions were rough. Before a battle, he would greet men by name instead of making speeches. To have one's exploit remembered by him was in itself an award, though his material rewards were generous. He was constantly interested in the common soldier's predicaments, however remote from his own.[9]

Leadership is not a position, but a relationship. As the story of Alexander illustrates, the relationship that inspires followers to great sacrifice is an intimate, caring connection. While Alexander was the supreme commander, he was in no way the autocratic bully. He terrorized his enemy, not his Companions. He was famous for his prebattle consultation with his officers. There was a formal leadership council, which also served as a way of unifying the diverse ethnic groups that formed his army.

After defeating the Persian Empire of King Darius, Alexander placed a number of Darius' more courageous generals in leadership positions in his own army. He pursued a vision of a united world and conveyed that vision with obvious symbolic acts. For example, he personally officiated at the wedding of nine thousand of his soldiers to Eastern women, the famous "marriage of East and West," symbolizing the unification of the conquered and conquering cultures.

But after his conquests, Alexander's personality changed, as often happens when a youth achieves great fame and fortune before maturity. He wandered with his massive army in pursuit of no particular goal. He was increasingly consumed by drink and conflicts created by competing lovers of both sexes. And in Egypt, where the idea of the "god-king" was long established, he discovered his own divinity. H. G. Wells writes:

> He was making no great roads, setting up no sure sea communications, forming no group of statesmen about him; he was thinking of no successor; he was creating no tradition—nothing more than a personal legend. The idea that the world would have to go on after Alexander, engaged in any other employment than the discussion of his magnificence, seems to have been outside his mental range. Whatever appearance of world-wide order may have gleamed upon men's imaginations, vanished at his death. The story becomes the story of a barbaric autocracy in confusion.[10]

It is not surprising that with Alexander's death, his empire collapsed. Just as Alexander was not the Prophet, the creator of the idea or innovation, neither was he the Builder nor Administrator needed to construct the mechanisms of organization and lasting civilization. He failed to recognize the higher level of challenge created by his own victories.

Alexander the Great, Attila the Hun, and many conquering entrepreneurs have a good deal in common. Barbarians all, they share a single-minded drive to achieve their goals. Many conquering entrepreneurs, while perfectly suited to command in the days of crisis, completely fail to recognize or rise to the subsequent challenges.

BUSINESS BARBARIANS: THE CLASH OF PERSONALITIES

In the world of business, as in history, a leader is a person with a clear sense of mission, strength, and urgency. Where historic Barbarians were always military commanders, the business Barbarian can emerge from almost anyplace in the organization. He may be the sales/marketing manager who has gained a larger vision, as did Ray Kroc when he came in contact with Mac and Richard McDonald. He may be the high-tech tinkerer, like Steven Jobs, who developed a passionate belief in the future of technology. Or he may be the financially skilled administrator who borrows, acquires, merges, and consolidates enterprises built by others, as did Frank Lorenzo of Texas Air. We know their names because of their ability to respond to challenges with decisive action. We have also seen the conflicts common to their typically short-lived reign of power.

Steven Jobs played the Barbarian to Stephen Wozniak's role of Prophet in the earliest days of Apple Computer. Jobs's "different" characteristics surfaced early. He lived on a fruit farm and later went to Tibet in search of the guru Neem Kardie Baba, a trip his companion described as "a kind of ascetic pilgrimage, except we didn't know where we were going."

In between he worked at Atari, and that experience, too, was different. Atari founder Nolan Bushnell remembers Jobs, who lacked any academic degree and little experience, would look over the shoulders of respected engineers and "regularly told a lot of them they were dumb shits."

Jobs explains this imperious nature of his Barbarian personality by saying: "Some of their engineers were not very good. The only reason I shone was that everyone else was so bad—I wasn't really an engineer at all."

Not surprisingly, Michael Moritz, in his excellent book *The Little Kingdom,* says that "the engineers didn't like Jobs. His unkempt appearance, and his belief that his fruit and yogurt diet meant that he could go without showers, didn't add to his popularity. Jobs's supervisor finally arranged for him to work late at night."[11]

Years later, as Apple Computer was adjusting to the requirements of mass production and marketing, Jobs knew very well that his personality was not the right one to handle more systematic pursuits. The success of Apple II had depended on his leadership and single-minded determination. So he placed himself in charge of the next developmental task, attacking the business office market dominated by IBM.

This assault may have begun when the blue-jeaned leader toured the Xerox research lab in Palo Alto, California, with his band of young revolutionary engineers. There they saw the new "mouse," similar to a Ouija board pointer, being used by an engineer. With millions of dollars and dozens of Ph.D. engineers, Xerox had been working to develop a system where all a user had to do was point the mouse at a series of "user friendly" icons, similar to cartoon characters, to get the computer to work. But despite all this effort, Xerox had not developed a product that anyone would buy, no matter what the price. As Jobs left the lab, he announced that within eighteen months he would produce a computer that would incorporate the same features and sell for around $3,000. the Ph.D.'s thought he was crazy. They didn't count on the revolutionary force of the Barbarian's will.

Jobs personally led the team that would develop the MacIntosh. He moved his Mac team into the simple, separate one-story building. He spent all his time with them, encouraging, demanding, criticizing, and praising. On more than one weekend when his team was hard at work, he dropped in to deliver envelopes containing stock options. Frustrated by slow progress on the chip for controlling sound, he told his two key engineers that he would remove the chip entirely unless it was operating correctly by Monday. The engineers labored through the weekend, and by Monday the sound worked perfectly. Every time Jobs asked, his team worked day and night until the task was completed. To immortalize his "Companions," Jobs had the signatures of all forty-five Mac group members embossed on the inside of the MacIntosh case.

Steve Jobs doesn't resemble our average corporate leader. Yet his behavior is entirely consistent with other youthful leaders of the past who overcame great odds and conquered new territory for their cause.

Jobs, Victor Kiam, and Ray Kroc were all Barbarian leaders who created successful enterprises. They all loved their product and were in touch with their people and production process. Each enjoyed living with their troops.

There is another type of Barbarian, however, more likely to come from the administrative side of enterprise than from marketing or production. While he may be equally aggressive, his impact will be very different.

Consider Frank Lorenzo. Lorenzo, chairman of Texas Air Corporation, acquired Eastern Airlines in the early 1980s, and it must have seemed a perfect fit. In 1987 there was only one airline that topped Lorenzo's Continental Airlines in complaints received by the Federal Aviation Administration. That company? Eastern. But this is what happens when employees don't get along with the people who pay them.

It is a simple fact that when employees feel alienated and angry at their leaders, they provide poor customer service. The customer walking onto the plane enters the airline's culture. Badly treated employees treat customers badly. This is a formula for competitive disadvantage, and nowhere is it more fully practiced than on Frank Lorenzo's airplanes.

Lorenzo is a case study in what can go wrong with a Barbarian personality, and like most who have created business empires, Lorenzo has a strong streak of Barbarianism. He definitely is a "get it done" kind of guy. He moved incredibly fast to consolidate airlines through his purchase of Continental, Frontier, People Express, and Eastern, and he brought down airline fares as a result of his cutrate competition. However, he has paid little attention to the quality of airline service provided by his airlines. That is understandable, given his background.

Trained at the Harvard Business School, and with no experience building new enterprises, he focuses his attention on finances: drive down costs, drive down prices, leverage the assets, and buy another airline. All his moves and management decisions are based on financial considerations, not customer needs. No vision of new or better products or services is emblazoned on a flag carried by his troops into battle. He lacks the nobler element of the Barbarian.

On a flight not long ago, I sat next to a TWA executive who reported his experience with Lorenzo. He had been recruited to join Texas Air during its earlier days.

"I was staying with Frank's partner. Lorenzo doesn't believe in getting personal with employees, even his top executives. When Frank came over after dinner, he asked if I wanted a drink. I said, 'Sure.' He asked if I drank martinis, and I said I did. And he said, 'Fine, I'll fix you one.' 'But,' I told him, 'I'd rather have a Scotch and water.'

"He turned and stared at me and said, 'I thought you said you drink martinis.'

" 'I do,' I answered, 'but I'd rather have a Scotch and water.'

"Then he said it again: 'I'll fix you a martini!'

"I couldn't believe it! I repeated my preference, but he just went ahead and fixed me a martini. I never drank it, I never joined his company. You see, Frank had to control the situation. He had to make sure that he could control others—he had to prove it."

It could be argued that Lorenzo's personality was exactly what was needed to consolidate the airlines into more efficient units. And he understands the acquisition game and plays it well. Yet Lorenzo, who has the determination and risk-taking disposition of the Barbarian, has not yet proved that he can manage either people or machines. He is only capable of manipulating debt and equity. The fact that he is in the airline business is merely coincidental. He could just as well be buying and driving down costs in any manufacturing or service company.

Lorenzo's reign may be shorter than Alexander's. For once assets are acquired, they must be made to perform. In a customer service business, the competitive advantage is the motivation and commitment of your employees. Now more than anything else, Lorenzo must change course. His airlines need the leadership that creates social purpose and unity. Perhaps he can change and become a leader of people rather than numbers. If he cannot, he will not last.

HOW TO GET ALONG WITH A BARBARIAN

If You Work for a Barbarian . . .

. . . be prepared for action. He will expect you to act quickly and not engage in lengthy or detailed planning exercises. Get to the heart of the matter and take action.

. . . do not expect to be involved in long meetings or consensus decision making. He'll make 'em—you'll carry 'em out!

. . . when he asks for your input, be completely honest and direct. Don't beat around the bush or give lengthy explanations.

. . . go to him, don't wait for him to come to you. If you want a promotion, a different job, or if you have an idea, you should seek him out and let him know about it in a straightforward manner. He may just say, "Okay, go do it."

If a Barbarian Works for You . . .

. . . be sure that his assignment is one where command and single-minded action are appropriate.

. . . leave no confusion about his area of responsibility and what you expect of him. If you do, he may get so far down the road so fast that you will have trouble getting things back under control.

. . . use him for what he is best at: turnaround situations, managing business units that are growing fast and need quick decisions. If your company is in decline and needs a revolution, put him in charge. He'll inject excitement and urgency and renew the vision.

. . . help the Barbarian make the transition to the next management stage by helping him involve his people more, delegate more, and consider longer-range factors and outcomes. With your help, he can probably make the transition.

THE BARBARIAN ORGANIZATION

The structure of an organization reflects its current challenges and the personality of the leader. In a Barbarian-led organization, that structure can be trying. For example, several years ago I was consulting with a successful local company. The president was the founder and had designed and sold the first product. As the company grew, he hired some professional managers who were becoming increasingly frustrated.

It was perfectly normal for the president to arrive at work at six A.M., spend an hour inspecting the product on the production floor, give instructions to the first employees as they arrived to begin their day, and not tell any of the other managers what instructions he had given. Why should he? It was his company. He had given birth to it. He knew more about the product than anyone else. They were his employees. He was in command.

He didn't have time or patience for what he regarded as the politics of the traditional organization. As a result, his subordinate managers, who recognized the intelligence and contribution of their leader, suffered. This is typcial.

The Barbarian tends to create an organization that suits his personality, rather than change his personality to meet the needs of the organization.

As organizations grow and mature, they differentiate, vertically by rank, horizontally by specialization. This process has just begun during the second, or Barbarian, stage of development.

But differentiation requires integration, administration, and consultation with others. These processes slow decision making and thus create a conflict with the personality of the Barbarian.

But that is not the only problem in a Barbarian-led organization. Systems are just being put into place, and the finances may not be in control. Also, there are not likely to be adequate methods of training, recruiting, appraisal, promotion, or discipline. Although you can be sure that the leader will have access to the information he needs, the information systems are likely to be crude.

The mental and emotional state of employees will parallel the state of the organization. Life is filled with great stress, excitement, and accomplishment. Every employee is likely to understand the mission and feel part of its achievement. The goal of the organization, like that of the leader, is simple and straightforward. The entire organization will focus on the two basics: the customer and the product or service. Everyone will complain that they are overworked.

But anyone who isn't overworked in a Barbarian Age organization doesn't understand the day in which he lives. The Barbarian leader will either wake him up or let him go. Paperwork should be kept to a minimum. Reporting should be face to face. There should be relatively few lines of approval. In this stage, no one has job descriptions. Everyone is too busy doing to sit down and figure out how each should complement and coordinate with others.

Precisely because of the rapid growth and likely disorder, the command decision-making style of the Barbarian is appropriate. If jobs are changing daily, there is no time to study "the best" way to organize the work. By the time the study is completed, the nature of the work has changed. Perfection can be pursued later. Now, it is more important to get the product out and close the sale.

CHALLENGES AND TASKS

Establishing a Secure Beachhead To be secure, a business must establish a territory and a reputation. To do that, the business Barbarian must develop a passion for satisfying the customer. Those who survive the early days of a business know that without this fundamental step, nothing else will follow.

In several presentations to graduate business school classes, I've asked: "What is the first thing you must have when you start a business?" Many of those students answer: "Create a strategic plan," or "A market study," or "Find capital." They are shocked when I tell them that the first and only thing they need is a customer! Most successful businesses were started without any plan, study, or much capital. They were started by people who knew they were in business, first and foremost, to serve a customer.

The base of repeat customers is the beachhead that must be established during the earliest days of a company. This is the number-one challenge of the Barbarian.

Discipline and Flexibility To win its first victory, the young organization must focus its energies. That requires discipline and consistency. Yet at the same time the young organization must be highly flexible. Changes in direction, personnel, and procedures will all have to be made rapidly. In order to accomplish both discipline and flexibility, decision making must rest with one or very few leaders.

Aged and bureaucratic organizations have lost both their flexibility and their discipline. As the organization becomes rigid and unresponsive, its members increasingly find ways to get around the formal systems. Revitalizing and transforming such an organization is a job for the Barbarian.

What I have to do is try to visualize the world, and I have to be agile enough to live with and win in it. It doesn't mean a thing to say I'm going to do so. It only means something to do it.

—JOHN F. WELCH, JR., CHAIRMAN, GENERAL ELECTRIC

Most large industrial corporations have grown bureaucratic. And General Electric was no exception. At the time Jack Welch took over as chairman, GE was ranked as the best-managed industrial company in the nation in a poll of Fortune 500 CEOs.[12] Apparently these CEOs were not well informed, because the new chairman immediately set in motion sweeping plans to redirect the business and change and renew the corporate culture.

Welch eliminated several layers of the GE hierarchy. He made extensive efforts to listen to the troops and get his subordinates to do the same, pushing decision making down along the management ladder to reduce response time. He cut costs by eliminating one hundred thousand jobs. Welch says he is "out to get a feeling and a spirit of total openness. That's alien to a manager of twenty-five to thirty years who got ahead by knowing a little bit more than the employee who works for him."

Welch's efforts appear successful so far. Profit and return on equity are up. And since 1981 GE's stock has risen more than twice as fast as the Standard & Poor's index of four hundred industrial stocks.

The questions for Welch are the same as for all Barbarians: What is the vision of the future that makes the present sacrifices worthwhile? Can a culture be developed in which people with a positive spirit are working toward positive goals? For Jack Welch, the question now becomes, can he give the employees of GE reason to believe that they are indeed "making the world a better place to live"?

Transforming Concepts into Action Entrepreneurial organizations frequently fail because their leaders are unable to distinguish between a great idea and a marketable product or service. Not every great idea is marketable. Fred Smith, founder of Federal Express, is a Barbarian who has given us illustrations of both how to succeed—and fail—in translating concepts into commercial products.

Smith developed the idea for Federal Express as a college student. He wrote a paper describing the idea of an overnight delivery service, where all packages would be sent to a single, centralized distribution center for sorting and dispatched to their destination in the middle of night. The paper received only a "C" from his professor, who told him it wouldn't work. But half a decade later, in 1971, he started Federal Express and set about proving, beyond any shadow of academic doubt, that his concept was sound.

Fred Smith's personality and his experience as a Vietnam fighter pilot were perfect for his task. According to his plan, every plane must leave at exactly the correct time each night to arrive in Memphis, where an army of young recruits works furiously to send the planes back out on their delivery mission. The Federal Express agents race to their destinations, running and panting, to make their 10:30 A.M. delivery deadline. It is this urgency and discipline that has won Federal Express a dominant market share.

Smith recognized that his own business was competing with modes of transmission that were even faster than overnight. He studied the ability of satellites to transmit information instantly and the growing use of Fax machines that transmitted letters over telephone lines.

This recognition led to the creation of Zap Mail. Federal Express would lease a dedicated satellite transponder, pick up letters from customers, and then instantly "zap" them to another city, where they would be delivered later that same day. Fred Smith loved the idea. Despite doubts from some of his most trusted advisers about the market for instantly "zapped" letters, he pushed its implementation. He leased the satellite at a cost of more than $100,000 a month. Zap pickup points were installed all over the country. Massive marketing began. There was one big problem:

little customer interest. Fred Smith had failed to anticipate that Fax could become an inexpensive method of instant transmission from one office to another. Zap Mail was a multimillion-dollar flop.

There are thousands of great ideas, but relatively few will ever lead to profitable businesses. A creative individual may come up with good ideas, but he is often the worst person to determine which can be transformed into a sound business venture. Barbarians are best when they are not so personally attached to the concept, when they can coldly assess the business potential.

Establishing a Performance-Oriented Culture Every organization during its early period establishes its culture, and like a growing child, habits and beliefs begin to take hold. While there is energy and flexibility, there is not yet the knowledge of what has worked in the past, the examples of heroes. It is during this Barbarian Age that leaders have the greatest opportunity to shape a culture that will produce maximum performance in the future.

Barbarians intuitively understand the importance of symbolic acts. It is for this reason that they will visit eight customers in one day and work until two in the morning to help get a product ready to deliver at seven. None of this is "their job," but they intentionally set the example of "doing what has to be done." Effective Barbarians work to create the company ethic by example.

It is difficult for managers raised in large corporations, where all activities are highly segmented, to break the mental restrictions about the roles of manager and employee. In the days when the culture is being formed, it is critical that the leader actually carry the sword into battle. He must not stand on the hill, aloof from his troops, and dispassionately give orders. The manager who insists on rigid and artificial distinctions between managers and workers is not the leader for the Barbarian Age. The Administrator will never create the legends, the heroic inspiration, or the values that will carry the company culture forward. To create such momentum, one must be a Barbarian.

Overcoming the Insensitivity of Command While the Barbarian is exactly the leader needed during the early days of an organization, some of his assets can quickly become liabilities. The Barbarian risks becoming habitually insensitive. He may become addicted to control and, by so doing, destroy the initiative and creativity of others. Or, like Alexander after all was won, he may not be able to change his focus and establish the necessary structures, systems, and specialization needed for the next stage of development.

There can be no question that Gen. George S. Patton possessed the qualities of decisive command so crucial in combat. Patton, a believer in reincarnation, also thought he was Alexander returned.

One day during World War II he was visiting an army field hospital, sitting beside his wounded troops to hear their stories of bravery, just as Alexander did. But that day Patton saw a young soldier who had been hospitalized for a nervous breakdown. Shouting that he would have no cowards in his army, he slapped the man. In order to march troops into battle even when the odds are unfavorable, the Barbarian must put aside normal sensitivities. For the Barbarian, the challenge is not to unleash his aggression in inappropriate circumstances.

That also often holds true in business. Yet once insensitivity is rationalized, a manager can quickly become accustomed to callousness, or worse, our Barbarian manager may have no one watching who can call him to account. If unchecked, the inevitable result will be loss of morale, and possibly the loss of good people. Either can cripple development of the next stage, which requires competent people to whom the leader can delegate.

New Challenge—No Complacency Another trap into which the Barbarian may fall is the complacency that results from the inability to recognize greater challenges. In his study of history, Arnold Toynbee pointed to several cultures, such as the Polynesians, who achieved a level of development and then stopped progressing because they were satisfied, unchallenged. This frequently happens in business. The entrepreneur develops a successful retailing concept but has no inclination to franchise or take the concept nationally.

Individuals can experience a plateau trap in their careers. Entire cultures can, too. Human ambitions are highly variable: not everyone wants to be Ray Kroc, builder of the McDonald's empire. One successful little restaurant can satisfy. It is the leader's ambition, his recognition and response to challenge, that determines whether growth is arrested at this stage.

◆

The Builder and Explorer

Specialization and Expansion

Insofar as a civilization grows and continues to grow, it has to reckon less and less with challenges delivered by alien adversaries and demanding responses on an outer battle field, and more and more with challenges that are presented by itself to itself in an inner arena. In other words, the criterion of growth is progress towards self-determination.

—ARNOLD TOYNBEE

The period of the Prophet may be a brief moment in the history of the corporation. The Age of the Barbarian should also be short. If an organization's leadership remains in the Barbarian Age, its growth will be arrested. It must move on and enter a period of specialization, a time when systems and structure take form, and the organization matures.

Now leadership has to take on a different character. It must be shared, delegated, and become increasingly collaborative. While the leaders must continue to be creative and fast moving, they must

59

also develop increasingly specialized competence in production, service, and sales. If they do, this third stage may last for centuries in the life cycle of a civilization and decades for a corporation.

The primary leaders in this period of specialization are the Builders and Explorers. The Builders will construct the internal means of efficient production, while the Explorers continue the push outward, expanding the boundaries of the developing corporation or culture.

A few years ago, People Express Airlines was featured in nearly every business publication. It was enormously successful. Its founder, Donald C. Burr, made the airline a model of participative management, employee ownership, and teamwork. But the glamour was short-lived. The company never could get beyond adolescence.

It suffered from the inflated ego common to overly successful youth. Addicted to the thrill of rapid growth, People Express acquired Frontier Airlines, paying far too much, and was not prepared to manage the integration of an alien culture. And it never did develop the specialized competence in planning and scheduling that are critical components of airline management. Without that specialized competence, the corporation could not survive, no matter how low its fares.

Swamped by debt and confused market strategies, People Express was finally saved only by its own surrender to Texas International.

But Donald Burr is not alone in his failure to make this critical transition from the entrepreneurial to the mature company. Thousands of enterprises have faltered at this stage, not recognizing the new demands that come with growth. Burr may consider himself in the company of Alexander, who also failed to make this transition.

In the first two stages of development, growth is highly dependent upon the individual leader, the Prophet and the Barbarian. But in the third stage, the environment—both internal and external—is becoming too complex for such centralized decision making.

Initially there was room for only one Mohammed, Buddha, or Attila on stage at any one time. But as society—or the company— matures, as the play becomes more complex, it becomes essential that many, perhaps less charismatic characters share the spotlight.

In the first two stages it was advantageous that the ego of the commanding leader expand to present a godlike appearance to his followers whose faith was required. Now humility and self-restraint are needed to promote collaboration and consensus.

The life cycle is never a perfect geometric curve. The actual progress of companies and civilizations is uneven, with flat periods of stagnation followed by sudden bursts of activity. Our own Western civilization is an example. Progress was promoted by the new Messiah and his devoted Apostles, who conquered Rome and the Greek world. But that progress came to an end with the Dark Ages and revived again during the Renaissance, when brilliant leaders, dedicated to their faith and their monarchs, developed new levels of specialized competence in the sciences, the arts, exploration, and commerce.

Similarly, the corporation may falter before entering this third stage of development. The Prophet or Barbarian may hold on too long. Henry Ford and his Barbarian Harry Bennett became addicted to power and control and were unable to develop a large and diversified company. In contrast, General Motors grew beyond dependence on any one personality and thrived as it built centers of specialization.

THE CHARACTER OF THE BUILDERS AND EXPLORERS

The Builder is in charge of getting the product produced or the service delivered to the customer. Traditionally he has matured with the organization. He remembers watching the product evolve from raw to finished goods. He has an immediate visual and tactile relationship to the work. Abstract concepts, plans, and strategies were the irrelevant preoccupations of persons who couldn't make anything.

While the Builder may still be in touch with the long-term vision of the Prophet, his orientation is generally short-term. What were the numbers yesterday, and what will they be tomorrow? It is not that he doesn't care about long-term interests, it is just that his thinking has been conditioned by years spent on the production floor.

Within every Builder is a strong component of the Barbarian. When managing a small production operation, where almost every Builder begins his career, you could lead by example. The production supervisor could show the worker exactly how the job was to be done. The supervisor could tell his employees to do something, and by God, they would do it! It felt good. And you didn't need a lot of systems and sophisticated administration to get things accomplished.

When the Builder is promoted above production to general management he enters a world where decisions are based on abstract issues, concepts, and strategies. He also enters a world that requires coordinated efforts between managers and groups with diverse interests, outlooks, and priorities. These "alien" views often sound like opposition or insubordination to the Builder, and he is likely to revert to his Barbarian style to overcome them. The promotion requires the Builder to think differently at an age when that change may be hard to come by.

The Explorer won't have that problem. He grew up in an entirely different world. A world where you could talk and persuade. The Explorer generally emerges from the selling organization and is likely to be an extrovert to the Builder's introvert.

The Explorer has no more fondness for administrative systems than the Builder. His "real work" is being out with the customer, getting him to buy. That is what it is all about! The Explorer has been highly successful at this. He has been repeatedly rewarded, not for sitting around in meetings in the home office, but for being out on the road, making the sale. His opinion of the "paper pushers" back home is not complimentary.

Business has only two functions, marketing and innovation.
—PETER DRUCKER

The nature of motivation changes in this stage. Personal rewards and luxuries are now available, and with their availability comes a question: What should inspire our leaders? Material wealth or serving mankind?

This conflict is present both in companies and civilizations. Western civilization entered its period of specialization around the sixteenth century, and you can see the conflict in a letter Christopher Columbus wrote after one of his voyages.

> So, since our Redeemer has given this victory to our most illustrious King and Queen, and to their famous realms, in so great a matter, for this all Christendom ought to feel joyful and make celebrations and give solemn thanks to the Holy Trinity with many solemn prayers for the great exaltation which it will have, in the turning of so many peoples to our holy faith, and afterward for material benefits, since not only Spain but all Christians will hence have refreshments and profit.[1]

As we are all prone to do, Columbus waxed eloquent on all of the noble benefits of his voyage, then slipped in the profit motive at the end, just in case his favorite sovereigns weren't in such a spiritual mood. Students of history have always debated the motives of the New World's explorers and conquerors, but it seems perfectly clear that both spiritual and materialistic motives were at work.

In the company, too, there will be twin motives. Some people will work in pure pursuit of the gold. Others will be focused solely on the Cause. The job of the leader is to work toward a balance of these motives. That balance will ultimately serve the expansion and progress of the company or civilization.

You May Be a Builder If . . .

. . . you enjoy the "real work" of your company, making the product or the delivery of the service.

. . . you enjoy measuring the results of your work.

. . . you like to make decisions quickly, take action, and see the results.

. . . you know you are not a visionary, and you don't waste a lot of time dreaming about the future.

. . . you don't like committees or sitting around wasting time talking.

You May Be an Explorer If . . .

. . . you are a convincing and enthusiastic communicator.

. . . you sometimes feel that you work for your customer, and others in your own company often seem to be obstacles to your goal of serving your customers.

. . . you love to keep score; you are competitive by nature.

. . . you believe your company should place a higher priority on expansion.

. . . you feel that your company gets bogged down in paperwork.

THE BUILDER AND EXPLORER IN HISTORY

If you ever doubt that man can act with courage of heroic proportions, you need look no further than the sixteenth-century explorers. Here were men who possessed not only great vision and courage, but great confidence in their ability to manage human affairs. Such a leader was Ferdinand Magellan. His story illustrates the combination of personal courage and competence, as well as the ability to communicate and cooperate, that are demanded in the Age of the Builder and Explorer.

Magellan was a Portuguese who, as a young man, served in his country's navy. At the time, ships en route to the Spice Islands sailed around Africa, but Magellan believed that a strait existed that would allow westward passage, and he wanted to find it. Portugal's king, Manuel, refused to fund a search, so on October 20, 1517, Magellan arrived in Seville to offer his services to Charles V, grandson of Ferdinand and Isabella, and the newly crowned King of Castile.

Charles, who had adopted the motto "Plus ultra," meaning "More beyond," ultimately accepted the offer. What kind of man had he decided to fund? Historian Edward G. Bourne summarized Magellan and his feat this way:

> There was none of the prophetic mysticism of Columbus in the make-up of the great Portuguese. Magellan was distinctly a man of action, instant, resolute, enduring. . . . The first navigation of the Straits of Magellan was a far more difficult problem of seamanship than crossing the Atlantic. . . . Columbus's voyage was over in thirty-five days; but Magellan had been gone a year and weathered a subarctic winter before the real task began—the voyage over a trackless waste of waters exactly three times as long as the first crossing of the Atlantic. . . . Magellan is to be ranked as the first navigator of ancient or modern times, and his voyage the greatest single human achievement on the sea.[2]

The Builder and Explorer stage of development is unlike the previous ones. Now the leader must gain the support and approval of others. Even then, there was a committee. It was the Casa de Contratacion, the official board that handled most of Spain's colonial affairs, similar to the corporate committees for capital authorization to which division managers must present expansion plans today. The Casa de Contratacion heard Magellan's plan but was unimpressed and denied approval.

Magellan then began lobbying to reverse the committee's decision. He sought the approval of Juan Foncesca, bishop of Burgos and the committee's most influential member. Foncesca sanctioned the voyage on the condition that his own relatives and favorites be made captains on Magellan's ships. There were three attempted mutinies during the trip, and historians suspect that those who tried to take over the expedition were acting with the bishop's encouragement.

Another member of the committee, Juan de Aranda, demanded a 20 percent cut of the expected profits in exchange for helping reverse the committee's vote. No Prophet or Barbarian could survive all the manipulation, coordination, and cooperation required of Magellan and other great Explorers in accomplishing their missions.

But accomplish it Magellan did. He sailed south and eventually found the strait that now bears his name. He circumnavigated the globe, uncertain where or when he might find a passage to the Pacific, totally ignorant of the immense size of that ocean, which is twice as large as the Atlantic, and without any of the navigational equipment we now take for granted. Magellan succeeded, not because he was simply courageous, but because he attended to all the details of keeping hour-by-hour logs, taking constant sightings of celestial bodies, and mapping every landfall and detail of the oceans he explored. He was not just visionary and courageous. He was also a technical genius.

While the Explorers were creating competitive advantages for their nations on the seas, the shipbuilders were also about to determine competitive advantage. The defeat of the Spanish Armada a few years after Magellan's conquest can be directly related to the failure of the Spanish to recognize the value of specialized competence. In 1588 Philip II, King of Spain, set as his personal mission the return of England to the Roman Catholic Church. Queen Elizabeth of England upheld Protestantism, the independence of England, and a growing secular tradition.

King Philip II almost never left his castle, even to witness the grand ceremony of the departure of his Great Armada. King Philip entrusted the execution of his mission to two dukes: the Duke of Parma, head of the King's land army in the Netherlands, and the Duke of Medina Sidonia, appointed Captain General of the High Seas, leader of the Armada, both of whom were to rendezvous and jointly invade England. The Duke of Medina Sidonia had no experience at sea or at war and pleaded with the King to appoint someone else. "Sir, in the interest of His Majesty's service, I submit to you, that I possess neither aptitude, ability, health nor fortune, for the expedition. The lack of any of these qualities would be enough to excuse me, and much more the lack of them all, which is the case with me at present."[3]

But the King was not listening. The two dukes were never able to consult with their king or each other and had entirely conflicting understandings of the plan.

During this period, ships of war were viewed merely as a means of transportation for the army and its general, not only by the Spanish, but by all nations. Sea captains and shipbuilders were entirely subservient to the land generals whom they served. The design of the Spanish ships was based on the tactics of land warfare in which the impenetrable castle and the high siege platform were considered of utmost importance. The Spanish ships were huge hulks built as high as possible so that soldiers could hurl arrows and spears down on their enemy. Because of the wind resistance to these sea castles, the Spanish fleet performed poorly to windward. When the Armada of one hundred and twenty ships left Spain, it encountered a northerly storm and made a pitiful fifteen miles' progress in three days. Within the first fifteen miles of the Great Armada's journey, the Spanish had already proven the virtual impossibility of defeating their enemy.

In England, where Queen Elizabeth was consulting with her naval experts, shipbuilding was taking a very different course. John Hawkyns, a former naval commander who had been routed by the Spanish early in his career, developed an entirely new view of the use of fighting ships at sea.

The ships built under the guidance of Hawkyns were built with the goal of windward performance and with only one purpose: to sail fast and maneuver nimbly, allowing the superior use of cannons and sea tactics to win the battle. He razed all castles off the ships, leaving only a low poop deck, lengthened the waterline, and narrowed the hull. He didn't care about cargo carrying ability; he would carry no soldiers. His ships lay "snug to the water." These ships were a daring innovation in the art of shipbuilding.

While Hawkyns was innovating with specialized ships, Sir Francis Drake, who had a close personal relationship with Queen Elizabeth, created the innovation of specialized command. Drake, also spurred by an encounter with the Spanish, established the principle of naval command, the captain of the ship as complete master of his vessel at sea. This specialized command structure was to become the key to the dominance of the British navy for several centuries.

As the Spanish Armada sailed up the English Channel, the Spanish generals expected the English to pull alongside their ships and engage in a battle of grappling hooks, archers, and boarding infantry. But the English never engaged in the Spaniards' battle. Holding the windward position, and always able to sail upwind of their enemy, Drake, Hawkyns, and the other English captains were in complete control of the battle strategy. They would attack when they found a few ships blown out of position and retreat when they were outgunned.

The passage of the Spanish Armada up the English Channel was one of the most humiliating military debacles in history. When the Armada reached the Netherlands, the Duke of Parma's army, unprepared, did not board the fleet. Many of the Spanish ships not bested in battle were torn by storms and washed ashore on the coasts of Scotland and Ireland, where the soldiers were mercilessly attacked by tribesmen. Only one-half of the Armada returned to Spain.

The victory of the English was not just a victory of courage and bravery. It was a victory of specialized technology and organization, a result of a recognized differentiation in competence between land and sea forces, tactics and equipment. England had entered the third stage of development, the dominance of the Builders and Explorers, the development of consultative leadership and differentiated organization. This acknowledgment of the necessity of specialized competence determined the fate of the Spanish Armada, the future of both Spain and England, Catholicism and Protestantism.

Magellan, Drake, and Hawkyns demonstrated all the qualities needed by leaders during this third stage of development. They must adhere to the strength of vision and values characteristic of the Prophet. And they must be able to take decisive action like the Barbarian. Yet there is also the absolute necessity of gaining the support of others, and even a willingness to compromise by accepting less than ideal conditions for the mission. Finally, there must be the expertise, the almost scholarly pursuit of technical competence, to drive the venture forward. Civilizations and corporations can expand successfully when they are blessed with leaders of such character.

THE BUSINESS BUILDERS AND EXPLORERS

The Builders and Explorers, the specialists in production and sales, are most responsible for the development of the large corporation. Their specialized organizations—and their ability to coordinate, consult, and cooperate—are the key leadership skills that result in growth. When these qualities are taken for granted, the culture, and the business, degenerate. When a bureaucratic organization is reinvigorated, it is these qualities that again become the dominant style of management.

The entire cycle can be observed in the Xerox Corporation. Chester Carlson, the inventor of xerography, was the Prophet who in 1938 created his first successful copier. For nine years he tried to sell his idea to more than twenty companies, including IBM, Kodak, and General Electric. They couldn't understand why anyone needed a machine to do what carbon paper did.

The heads of America's largest companies might not have been able to understand the significance of Carlson's invention, but Joe Wilson did.

Wilson's Haloid Company was an insignificant Rochester, N.Y.– based firm until it discovered Carlson's work. Wilson played Barbarian to Carlson's Prophet. He funded the research to develop xerography and is primarily responsible for transforming research that was almost ignored into one of the most successful products and companies in business history.

But the great success of Xerox was not only its technology, but the drive to see it to market. Its success is also based on the ability to design and manufacture a reliable product. The 914 copier worked. Some are still working thirty years after Horace Becker, the man insiders call the father of the 914, designed them.

"I am not an inventor," says Becker, who managed the engineering and manufacturing of the 914. "I understand what is required to take a concept and help make it a commercial reality."[4] The genius of what Becker did was to take an extremely complex technology, incorporate it into a reliable machine, and make it simple to use. All you had to do was push the button. Anyone could operate the 914 copier.

Complex technology made simple to use created a revolution in information handling. Becker's contribution was the obsessive attention to every detail of the design and production process. Becker, who would become Xerox's vice president of engineering, was the Builder who made the machine work.

Xerox's success is also attributable to innovative marketing. The company understood that a unique product required a unique approach to the market. A new challenge requires a new response.

Because the copier was unfamiliar, office managers could not have justified the purchase price to their superiors, even if they believed in its value. So rather than sell the copiers, Joe Wilson leased them. In fact, he priced them so people would want to rent. Though the copiers cost $2,000 each to build, the initial price of the 914 was $29,500. It originally leased for $95 a month with the first two thousand copies free. It turned out the per-copy charge after two thousand copies generated more than the monthly rent. In 1967 each 914 brought in $4,500. This meant that Xerox recouped all of its investment in production and marketing during the first year. Everything after that was profit, and there was a great deal after that.

Carlson, Wilson, and Becker are the heroic characters of Xerox's youth. They represent the invention, vision, drive to action, and technical competence. They allowed Xerox, as Wilson eventually renamed his company, to grow beyond anyone's greatest expectations. But with that growth came problems.

The office copier business became so large, and Xerox had such a huge share of it, that in 1972 the Federal Trade Commission accused Xerox of illegally monopolizing the market. SCM, another office equipment manufacturer, sued Xerox for antitrust violations. IBM sued. These attacks made Xerox far more conservative than it had been. Company leaders became afraid to act and relied more and more on their attorneys. Lawyers checked every speech and memo. When executives met with other companies to discuss possible deals, the lawyers were present. The bureaucratic culture of caution and control was taking over.

The results were seen quickly. By the time David Kearns became chairman in 1980, "we were horrified to find that the Japanese were selling their small machines for what it cost us to make ours. Our costs were not only way out in left field, they weren't even in the ballpark. Let me tell you, that was scary, and it woke us up in a hurry."[5]

During the past several years Xerox has rebounded, recapturing huge chunks of market share—as much as 14 percent in one year—and reestablishing itself as the dominant force in the copier business. What changed? A realization of the need for excellence in design, engineering, and manufacturing. The very things that made Xerox great initially.

Every one of Xerox's one hundred thousand employees has gone through forty-eight hours of quality training. Every employee is now a participant on a team that tracks and monitors quality, seeking continuous improvement. "Just in time" manufacturing procedures, which eliminate incoming inventory and inspection, has reduced inventories and costs and forced Xerox to develop closer supplier relationships. Computer-added design and manufacturing has been used to help develop the most recent copiers.

The emphasis is again on building the best possible machine. Listen to Wayland Hicks, who at the age of forty became head of copier development and production for Xerox in 1983:

> I wanted to make this company even more entrepreneurial. Break it down into groups of four, five, and six. Give them bonuses. Give them incentives. Make everyone profit-oriented. . . . Then, maybe I could get rid of the constant bickering between engineering and manufacturing. When a problem comes up, one side blames the other. The engineers say it's a manufacturing problem and the manufacturing guys say, "Look at the designs we have to work with." I don't really give a damn about manufacturing or engineering. I just care about what's good for the company and I want those guys to think that, too.[6]

Actually, the portrait of Hicks in *Xerox: The American Samurai*, demonstrates that he cares a great deal about manufacturing and engineering. Hicks and others like him have succeeded in creating and holding market position because they possessed the vision of the Prophet, the decisive action orientation of the Barbarian, and an appreciation for technical achievement. This is the Builder.

HOW TO GET ALONG WITH BUILDERS AND EXPLORERS

If You Work for a Builder . . .

. . . you should have clear and specific written objectives. He hates surprises and believes that you should have a blueprint for your activities.

. . . you have probably noticed that he isn't the world's greatest communicator. You can help him by initiating needed communication. Don't expect him to.

. . . don't expect a great deal of positive reinforcement. He takes satisfaction from the quality and volume of product going out the door, and he expects you will, too.

. . . he appreciates creativity within bounds. He appreciates better ways to get things accomplished. He is more interested in "how to" than "what to or why to."

If a Builder Works for You . . .

. . . be sure that your measurement and feedback is not based entirely on the short term. He already tends in that direction. You need to help him think long term.

. . . he may not understand the need for involving people below him in decision making.

. . . don't reward him for results. Reward him for improving processes.

. . . don't burden him with a lot of central staff help. He likes to run his own operation with the greatest-possible degree of autonomy. Hold him accountable for improvements and offer help. Don't impose it.

If You Work for an Explorer . . .

. . . you will win points for results and gaining new business, things Explorers understand most.

. . . he wants to hear about your plans. He wants to know that you have high objectives and expectations.

. . . he doesn't like to hear about what can't be done, might go wrong, or should have been done. He is sensitive to the level of enthusiasm.

If an Explorer Works for You . . .

. . . he appears to need your approval more than others. He is out in the wilderness most of the time. When he comes back to the home office he needs your praise. Let him have it.

. . . he is likely to be overly optimistic about his own performance. Don't shoot him down. Help him to develop more realistic expectations and projections.

. . . he will want you to spend more time in the field with customers than you can afford. Work with him on making the best use of his time.

. . . he probably doesn't have the best relations with those whose support he needs in the home office or in production. Help him to understand the importance of these members of his team.

THE ORGANIZATION OF THE BUILDER AND EXPLORER

This stage will be characterized by the development of increasingly specialized skills, resulting in an increasingly differentiated organization. Marketing will become distinct from selling, so there will now be a marketing department along with a sales department.

Production engineering will become distinct from production management, and two separate divisions will be created.

Along with this separation of function—a horizontal division within the company—comes vertical differentiation as well. In this phase we see a separation on the basis of rank.

You can see this division simply by looking at the kind of building that houses the organization.

The new entrepreneurial company is likely to have a one-story building with few differences in office size or furnishings. The organization is simple and so is the building that it calls home.

But as it enters the third stage of development, the building, like the organization, becomes more complex. The building grows taller, and the status of the occupant can be determined by the size, building material, and ornamentation. There are also specialized rooms.

The divisions of specialized labor are essential to gaining the competitive advantages of efficiency, mass production, and distribution. During this third stage there is increasingly sophisticated competition, and the battle will be won less as a result of innovation and more as a result of improvements in quality and cost. The increasingly specialized structure is a response to this challenge.

But with this specialization comes a loss in social unity. During a company's early days, when it is fighting to survive, unity is almost assured. People are working together with a common purpose.

But now people are being separated by function. The broad mission is no longer obvious to the manager working in one of the many production departments. He or she is fulfilling only a small piece of that which leads to progress toward the collective social mission. The very glue that held society together, while still present, has begun to give way to individualism.

Universities are a good example of this. First, there is a college of humanities. It houses all learning of human history and nature. Then there is the division of history and social sciences. Then, within the social sciences, the division of psychology and sociology. They form their own departments, academic societies, and journals. Then, within psychology, there is the division of animal behavior and human behavior. Then the division of humanistic, analytic, and behavioral psychology, each with its own—even more specialized—journal and organization.

This specialization is useful in focusing research on specific problems. But in time, the fields of knowledge will become so narrow as to become increasingly unimportant and detached from any larger social purpose.

In an educational environment, this may be acceptable. Integration is not an obvious requirement for research and study. In the corporation, however, the failure to integrate knowledge and skills results in automobiles designed by isolated engineers who do not regard production as their concern and studies by the marketing department that do not meet the needs of the sales force. Production managers then curse the designers for blueprints that make it impossible to build reliable cars, and the sales force curses the marketing department for irrelevant information and strategies. The social glue easily comes undone.

Maintaining social purpose and unity now requires deliberate action by the leaders. The company must integrate technology, skills, markets, finance, and communications. The leader must talk to all competing forces within and help them recognize their interconnection and interdependence.

Harvard University professors Paul R. Lawrence and Jay W. Lorsch[7] studied the nature of differentiation and integration. Their conclusions are entirely consistent with an analysis of how civilizations handle the same tasks.

Lawrence and Lorsch point out that specialization means not only organizational differentiation, but differences in attitude and behavior, in organizational culture. And the greater the organizational differentiation, the more divergent the attitudes and the more difficult integration becomes.

They theorized that high-performing organizations would have levels of differentiation appropriate to their environment *and* comparably effective integration.

They tested their theory by looking at six chemical companies. They found that the two organizations with the best performance records had, in fact, achieved the highest degree of integration. They were also among the most highly differentiated. The two lowest-performing organizations were neither highly differentiated nor well integrated.

Furthermore, successful integration was found to be directly related to a manager's ability to deal effectively with interdepartmental conflicts. In the best-performing organizations, managers were able to resolve conflicts between people with differing orientations.

The new company is likely to have only one or two customers, or one or two types of customers, and therefore require little specialization. There is little need for delegation, cooperation, or integration, so the commanding style of the Barbarian may succeed.

But as the company matures, it starts to develop diverse products, which attract diverse clients. As this process continues, increasing skill and organization differentiation results. This calls for a higher level of integration.

Growth that leads to differentiation often decreases quality. Managers, obsessed with increasing production, continue to isolate individuals and functions in the name of efficiency, eroding motivation, and responsibility. The employee loses track, forgets that he is serving a customer.

Surprisingly, Toynbee is able to trace this process back as far as 1425 B.C.

> The handiwork of "Late Minoan III" falls below that of the preceding phases of Minoan culture in standard of workmanship and in artistic power as conspicuously as it outranges all previous Minoan handiwork in its geographic distribution. In this Minoan instance, it looks almost as if the deterioration in the quality of craftsmanship was the price which had to be paid for an expansion of "output"; and the moment at which this apparent sacrifice of quality to quantity was made seems to be coincident with the beginning of the end of the Minoan Civilization.[8]

At every stage of development there is conflict within the organization as well as conflict with the external environment. During the third stage, however, this conflict becomes increasingly internal.

There is both a natural alliance and a natural conflict between Builder and Explorer, and this push and pull will dominate the organization during its third stage.

The sales organization must rely upon the production department and therefore wants them to succeed. However, many of the problems presented to the sales and marketing people will be caused by the production department.

The customer will point to flaws in the product and yell, "You sold me that!" And the salesperson will curse the production manager under his breath.

The Builder, on the other hand, will feel as if he is working for the salespeople, always trying to meet schedules, making the product in a unique color or size to meet a customer's demands. Yet he is being reprimanded for defects that this customization brings.

This conflict is consistent with the fact that the challenge the organization now faces comes from within, and the managers who oversee the two warring departments probably are having problems of their own dealing with the fact that the organization has changed and a new management style is needed.

In the first two stages of development, as we have seen, the company is worried about survival. Now it is worried about how to do things better.

This change in focus forces the company to adopt a new management style. Since the greatest expert on marketing one of the company's many products may be three layers below the top executive, relying on centralized decision making no longer makes sense. The centralized leader is too far removed to make effective decisions.

Delegation, and the development of consensus or group decision making, is now the only method of creating effective decisions that integrate the knowledge of various specialized experts.

That makes sense. But it is often difficult for the successful Prophet or Barbarian to make that change.

The shift in management decision-making style is not unlike the changes in parenting style that occurs as the child progresses from childhood to maturity.

As parents of young children know, direct orders often work

best. "You will finish your vegetables, and then you may have dessert."

But while the five-year-old needs clear direction and the immediate rewards and applause, the same approach with an adolescent is likely to result in rebellion and animosity. Command must give way to consultation. Now the parent must become the counselor, listening and recommending, encouraging and suggesting. He may only resort to commands in a crisis.

The same holds true of managers in the third stage, and, like parents, they find it hard to make the shift. They try to keep the decision-making function centralized and thereby retard their people and organization.

Your Organization Is in the Building and Exploring Age If . . .

. . . your products or services have proven to have a competitive advantage and you are growing rapidly.

. . . you are now profitable and can afford to add needed staff, and you are developing management systems.

. . . you are hiring more, and the jobs are becoming more specialized.

. . . there is high confidence in the future.

CHALLENGES AND TASKS OF THE BUILDING AND EXPLORING STAGE

The period of building and exploring may be the best of times in the corporation. There is still the opportunity and excitement of growth, and the ills of age are not present. Managers are now confident that they are headed in the right direction.

Their challenge is to help the corporation mature without losing the energy and creativity of youth. As we have seen, they must develop an organization where the jobs are clearly differentiated, but the corporation remains unified.

Redefining the Market and Securing
Market Position

Armed with an innovative product or service, a new company targets a specific, and often narrow, market. But an innovation is only an innovation for a short period of time. The challenge now is to fulfill the potential of the product and to find ways to expand.

During this stage of development there will be an inevitable tension between those who want to devote all of the organization's resources to the primary product and those who want to diversify. The argument may be as simple as whether all Model T's should be black, or should McDonald's stick solely to hamburgers and french fries. There is opportunity for growth, if we diversify a bit, says one faction. Why diversify when we are so successful in this market, which we still have not fully exploited? says the other. These debates often result in the leaders of the old order giving way to the leaders of the new.

Reducing Unit Cost, Increasing Quality

Product innovations don't last forever. Eventually competitors catch on and respond with similar products and services of their own. Once the innovative advantage is gone, the business must compete on cost and quality. It is during this third phase that money and energy must be invested in efficiencies. This is an investment many companies are reluctant to make. Experiencing profit for the first time, they are lulled to sleep at exactly the moment they should be living in fear of competition and spending their money to gain production and marketing advantages.

The Challenge of Competence

Specialization requires higher skills. The more specialized the tasks of a job, the less likely it is that the organization will have someone on staff who can do it. Because the organization is rapidly growing, and its functions are becoming more specialized, its superiority can only be maintained if it focuses on the development of its people. This requires an emphasis on both superior recruitment and training.

Both Builders and Explorers tend to be focused on the "here and now." They need to get the product out and reach the customer right this minute! That is understandable. Yet the long-term competitive advantage of the organization depends upon its ability to maintain human superiority. The pattern of human development is established during this third stage, and that pattern will be a major indicator of how well the organization will do in the future.

Developing Staff and Administration

The rapidly growing firm is a delicate balance of forces. In this stage of development the manager most likely to rise to head the organization will probably come from either sales or production. His background will dictate his feelings about what the "real work" of the organization is.

If he is from sales, he will talk about the company as a "marketing driven company" while failing to truly understand that he is now responsible for manufacturing as well.

If he is from the production or scientific side, he will talk about becoming the "technology leader" or the "lowest cost producer."

An effectively managed company is somewhat like a flying bird, the two wings being the sales/marketing side and the production/service side. If either wing falters, the bird crashes. It is the job of the executive to keep both wings in perfect balance and to allow for his biases.

The easiest way for the manager to keep the necessary balance is to develop an effective administrative structure, one that consistently provides him with the information he needs to spot when the company is tilting too far. Yet this too is alien to our manager. During this period it is still people with functional skills—sales or production—who dominate the organization, and neither side has much use for "paper pushers" who develop systems.

The danger now is that the production and sales managers who emerge as leaders during this period will neglect the development of the administrative functions at exactly the stage when they must be developed if the organization is to continue its growth.

Managing Expectations

At this stage of development the organization is riding a wave of high expectations. Growth has resulted from good decisions, but success may blind the leaders to the risks of failure.

If the founder is the major owner of the corporation, it is entirely possible that all of his expectations have been met by the company's success. His net worth may now be more than he ever dreamed possible. And we know that neither people, civilizations, nor companies make major leaps forward when they are satisfied. As Toynbee said, "Ease is inimical to civilization," and the key individuals in the organization may be experiencing ease for the first time. Ironically, this success can destroy the company.

If the organization is dominated by the founder, the almost inevitable changing of his personality is sure to affect the company's culture. People respond to success in strange ways. Some founders begin to think of themselves as "big executives" and their companies as major corporations. They attempt to conform to stereotypes that are inherently destructive.

Once successful, one company founder with whom I am familiar started to look for similar companies to acquire. The fact that he was pursuing the acquisition of inefficient companies at unwarranted prices and assuming unrealistic debt loads was not important to him. He believed this was the way the "big business game" was played, and he felt ready to play. He ended up acquiring companies larger than his own, ones he could not manage. The result? Several years of multimillion-dollar losses and his eventual ouster as CEO. He didn't know when he had it good.

Other managers quickly take on Hollywood's version of the corporate executive's life-style. There are chauffeurs, airplanes, and country club memberships. Again, they think this is the way executives are supposed to behave. They are setting a bad example for their employees, and they are corrupting their own character in a way that guarantees their own loss of creativity.

The growth of the organization at this point depends upon the ability of its managers to continue to develop creative responses to new challenges. Success can destroy creative energy.

The CEO/founders who are to be most admired are those who maintain their creative performance and enjoy the fruits of their success, but in moderation. This life-style, not portrayed on television, is more typical of the genuinely excellent corporation executive. The days of tycoons are over.

◆

The Administrator

Systems, Structure, and Security

Whenever an individual or a business decides that success has been attained, progress stops.

—THOMAS WATSON, SR.

There's no resting place for an enterprise in a competitive economy.

—ALFRED P. SLOAN

The territory conquered, the markets won, production under way, now administration is called for.

During the second stage of development, the Barbarian initiates simple forms of administration, keeping track of performance, counting territory conquered. But there is no need for complex administrative systems, no department of planning or personnel. During the period of the Builder and Explorer, in which specialization of functions and organizations develop, the need for administration is on the rise. Initially, administration serves the needs of those producing and selling, building and exploring. But gradually the tide turns, and it appears that those producing and selling increasingly come to

83

serve those administering. And it is the turning of this tide that signals the entry into the Administrative stage.

In this fourth stage, the corporation is holding its ground, creating and maintaining order. And now the successful leaders face their single greatest test. Are they able to maintain forward motion, continue to be creative, decisive, and develop increasing competence, while at the same time administering secured territory? If they can, the organization will break through to that ideal synergy that assures continued health. If they can't, and the Administrator becomes dominant, decline will begin. There is an inherent conflict between the creative impetus to growth and the need for order. In this stage of a company's evolution, order is increasingly the victor.

To survive this stage, managers must understand the difference between leadership and management. Leadership provides the vision, values, and purpose that creates motion. Management channels the energy leadership creates. Leadership is necessarily personal; administration is necessarily impersonal. In order to inspire followers and engender their loyalty, leadership must appeal to intuition and emotion. Administration appeals to the rational intellect with facts and numbers.

We elected Ronald Reagan and rejected Jimmy Carter precisely because of these distinctions. Reagan is not famous for his command of numbers, information, and facts. Carter was respected for his exhaustive information gathering and command of details. He was a strong Administrator. These abilities were—perhaps rightly—admired by many people. However, Ronald Reagan is regarded as a more successful "leader," although clearly a less able Administrator. Reagan did what leaders must do. He presented a positive vision of the future for the people he sought to lead. He described his vision with enthusiasm. He engendered confidence. There is a positive dynamic energy between leader and follower that has absolutely nothing to do with facts or numbers. But in the Administrative Age, energy is gradually overcome by the minds filled with numbers.

THE CHARACTER OF THE ADMINISTRATOR

The Administrator's view of corporate performance is far different from the one held by leaders in the first three stages.

The Prophet viewed performance as derived from creation; the Barbarian from decisive action; and the Builder and Explorer from specialized competence and coordinated effort. The Administrator in control believes that order and systems will result in performance. The Administrator may spend more of his time focusing on how things are done rather than what or why things are done. He spends more time with financial reports than with customers. His focus is on what has happened, calculating past results rather than developing a vision of what he intends to make happen in the future. He reacts rather than acts.

Is this a problem? Military history has repeatedly proved that the decision to assume a defensive posture, to merely hold territory, is the decision that eventually leads to defeat.

The development of administration can best be observed in the expansion of the American railroads. The railroads were the prototype of the modern American corporation. They were the first to require coordination of resources and schedules across a large territory and thus demanded great numbers of full-time managers. It was these railroad managers who first developed what we regard as modern administrative practices to coordinate, control, and evaluate the activities of scattered operating units. The resulting efficiencies, later adopted by the nation's production and service organizations, are largely responsible for the global expansion of large corporations over the past century.

The impact of transportation on the culture and commerce of a nation cannot be overstated. Up until the nineteenth century, the speed and reliability of transportation had not increased much since the time of Christ and the Roman legions. Travel by foot, cart, horseback, or sailing ship remained the only alternatives. It is doubtful that the average rate of transport had increased one mile per hour over the two thousand years prior to the advent of the railroad. The steam engine of Scotsman James Watt would change commerce and the world forever—and nowhere more rapidly than in the huge territory of the United States.

In the United States, once uniform standards, methods of construction, grading, tunneling, and bridging were developed, railroads expanded rapidly. The number of vehicles, miles of track, and requirements for maintenance and safety all demanded careful coordination. Such coordination required consistent information and uniformity. In short, the expansion of the railroads required administration.

It was not a single Barbarian who conquered the territory of the United States with steel rails, but rather several men, each with his own regional company, who collectively conquered all other means of transportation within a few short years. In the 1840s only four hundred miles of new canals were built, bringing the nation's total to just under four thousand. During that same decade, the innovative railroads put into operation over six thousand miles of track, bringing the total to nine thousand miles by 1850.[1] By 1860 railroads had replaced canals and waterways as the primary means of transportation.

The process of specialization and integration that characterizes the growth of civilizations can also be seen in the development of the railroads. Following their rapid growth, the railroads began to merge. The various lines along the Erie Canal and Hudson River were consolidated in 1853 to form the New York Central. That integration required even more specialized administrative control. Daniel C. McCallum of the Erie was promoted to general superintendent of the new line and charged with creating a smoother-running organization.

McCallum first prescribed a set of "general principles" of administration as follows:

1. A proper division of responsibility.

2. Sufficient power conferred to enable the carrying out of responsibilities.

3. The means of knowing whether such responsibilities are faithfully executed.

4. Great promptness in the report of all derelictions of duty, that evils may be at once corrected.

5. Such information to be obtained through a system of daily reports and checks that will not embarrass principal officers nor lessen their influence with their subordinates.

6. The adoption of a system, as a whole, which will not only enable the General Superintendent to detect errors immediately, but will also point out the delinquent.[2]

McCallum's system worked. In 1854 the *American Railroad Journal* reported:

> By an arrangement now perfected, the superintendent can tell at any hour in the day, the precise location of every car and engine on the line of the road and the duty it is performing. Formerly, the utmost confusion prevailed in this department, so much so, that in the greatest press of business, cars in perfect order have stood for months upon switches without being put to the least service, and without its being known where they were. All these reforms are being steadily carried out as fast as the ground gained can be held.[3]

Who can argue with success? Who would deny McCallum the full credit he deserves for creating the administrative systems that would enable the development of commerce and civilization across the continent? We should give credit to all administrators who provide the systems that enable efficient operations in all of our companies. Yet at the same time, we should recognize the seed of decline in the very pronouncement of triumph in the above report. That seed lies in the last phrase of the *Railroad Journal*'s glowing narration: "as fast as the ground gained can be held." It is not Barbarians or Builders and Explorers who have a passion for holding ground. It is the province of the Administrator to secure and hold territory, to make it safe and orderly, to create conditions of greater comfort and safety. All desirable conditions, true, but conditions that can lead to rigidity. And as history stands ready to testify, these very conditions have proved contrary to the growth that necessitated administration in the first place.

Business historian Alfred D. Chandler, Jr., points out that this consolidation strategy was essentially defensive:

> The formulation of the strategies that created these "megacorps" indicates much about the motives of the managers, investors, and speculators who guided the destinies of American railroads. The systems were not built to reduce costs or increase current profits. The strategies of growth were not undertaken to fill any need for or to exploit the opportunities resulting from improved administrative coordination. By the 1880s such coordination had already been achieved for the American railroad network through inter-firm cooperation. The basic motive of system-building was, therefore, defensive.[4]

In time the administrative procedures that had been so helpful to the railroads came to stifle progress and creativity. And the developing railroad bureaucracy would soon see a reaction in the form of unions. The unions created a bureaucracy at the bottom to match that at the top, and the entire culture became as rigid as the rails. This rigidity fixed the business in structures and systems that would soon become a brake on expansion. It is the rigidity of thought, begun in this period, that prevented the leadership from creative responses to new challenges.

You May Be an Administrator If . . .

. . . you have risen in the corporation's staff organizations.

. . . you consider yourself expert at the procedures, processes, and systems of management.

. . . order, consistency, and smooth operations are high priorities for you.

. . . you devote more time to checking on what has happened, as reflected in financial reports, for example, than you spend focused on future growth in products, service, or customers.

THE ADMINISTRATOR IN HISTORY

In the development of civilizations, the Administrative stage can be identified by the change from offense to defense—the shift from outward to inward focus—which coincides with the achievement of affluence. Both the Roman Republic and the later Roman Empire experienced periods of expansion, followed by a defensive period, which resulted in decline. The Roman Republic was at its spiritual peak in the third and fourth century B.C. At the time, the Roman assembly was the most democratic and vital ruling body the world had ever seen, leading the republic into a period of relative peace and prosperity. But gradually the Romans' inward focus led to a complacency that took for granted the values and virtues upon which their democratic process was constructed.

Two of the most significant and decisive military campaigns in Roman history illustrate the gradual shift in thinking and the change in culture within the cornerstone institution of that civilization, the Roman legions.

Around 300 B.C., Carthage was the dominant empire of the West. Like most dominant empires, she had tributary states that did not love her and a large and disloyal internal industrial slave population. Rome was youthful and innovative. The Carthaginian navy had ruled the Mediterranean for two hundred years, and her generals considered their dominance of the sea the natural order. The leading Carthaginian battleship was a "quinquereme," a large galley with five banks of oars, which could ram or shear the oars off a smaller vessel. When the Romans began expanding southward and entered into war with Carthage, they had no comparable battleships.

However, two months following their first naval battle Rome built one hundred quinqueremes. More important, they had discovered a way of boarding the boats of their enemy. They devised a long drawbridge on their ships, held up by a mast and pulley. They also loaded their ships with soldiers. As the Carthaginians rammed or swept alongside, this devise was lowered and Roman soldiers swarmed aboard. This simple innovation was enough to turn the tide in the war between the old empire and the new republic. In just a few years Carthage became an "estate" of Rome.

Between the defeat of Carthage and the defeat of the Roman legions under Crassus at Carrhae in 53 B.C., a major shift occurred in the entire Roman culture. Rome had become more concerned with its internal affairs—finance and personal gain—than with expansion and the unification of its people.

As H. G. Wells points out:

> After the fall of Carthage the Roman imagination went wild with the hitherto unknown possibilities of finance. Money, like most other inventions, had "happened" to mankind, and men had still to develop—to-day they have still to perfect—the science and morality of money. What had happened to Rome? Various answers are made —a decline in religion, a decline from the virtues of the Roman forefathers, and the like. We, who can look at the problem with a large perspective, can see that what had happened to Rome was "money." Money had floated the Romans off the firm ground.[5]

Other changes in the Roman culture also occurred symptomatic of maturing cultures. The soldiers, once common citizens serving temporary duty as an act of loyalty, became a professional class, recruited from the poor and conquered, held together by recompense rather than social purpose. Farmers who once plowed their own land employed a growing class of slaves. The Senate became increasingly populated by the wealthy or those serving the wealthy. The common people were beginning to become alienated and distrustful. Yet to an outside observer, the body of the republic appeared increasingly strong. The physical territory and material assets were still growing. But the spirit was not.

In 53 B.C. Crassus, known as a great money lender and war

profiteer, led the Roman legions against the Scythians, a tribal people who were skilled horsemen. The Scythians lured the legions into an area of hot sand, and through two days of battle, the Romans, who believed they, more than any other people, had perfected the art of warfare, attempted to charge the circling cavalry. The Scythians on horseback easily evaded the Roman foot soldiers, all the while sending arrows raining into the Roman ranks. Twenty thousand Romans died. Another ten thousand marched into slavery.

The significance of Crassus' defeat at Carrhae was the inability of the Roman military to respond creatively. Confronted by overwhelming Scythian might, the Romans mechanically relied on their proven methods, despite the obvious presence of a new challenge. Growth and expansion continue as long as the leaders are creative in the presence of a new challenge. When they begin to rely on yesterday's successful response, the decline has begun.

Even after the defeat, the Roman Empire continued to grow and reached its peak in physical size under Trajan (A.D. 98) after he annexed Armenia, Assyria, and Mesopotamia. But the decline was already under way.

Trajan was succeeded by Hadrian, best known for his building of Hadrian's wall in Britain (a testament to the transition from an expansive to a defensive posture), designed to hold back the dreaded "barbarians." Hadrian was reportedly of a "cautious and retractile disposition," and he was soon replaced by another administrative Caesar, Marcus Aurelius Antoninus.[6]

Historian F. W. Farrar paints the picture of a dedicated administrator:

> He [Marcus Aurelius] regarded himself as being, in fact, the servant of all. The registry of citizens, the suppression of litigation, the elevation of public morals, the care of minors, the retrenchment of public expenses, the limitations of gladiatorial games and shows, the care of roads, the restoration of senatorial privileges, the appointment of none but worthy magistrates, even the regulation of street traffic, these and numberless duties so completely absorbed his attention that, in spite of indif-

ferent health, they often kept him at severe labor from early morning till long after midnight. His position, indeed, often necessitated his presence at games and shows; but on these occasions he occupied himself either in reading, or being read to, or in writing notes. He was one of those who held that nothing should be done hastily, and that few crimes were worse than waste of time.[7]

No one questions the sincerity and good work of Marcus Aurelius. He was dedicated to improving the order of the empire, to serving his people. He was not, however, dedicated to expanding, creating, or building.

With the death of Marcus Aurelius, the period of unity and comparatively good government in the Roman Empire came to an end. Marcus Aurelius' own son, Commodus, inaugurated an age of bureaucracy and disintegration. Now the Caesars did little governing. They played at aristocratic games and left the efforts to control the empire to a class of professional bureaucrats. For the next one hundred years, a succession of emperors wrote their history of internal criminality, while outer defenses began to fall under the pressure of a simpler and more energetic people, the "barbarians."

BUSINESS ADMINISTRATORS

As the corporation achieves size and security in its market, it develops the structure, systems, and staffs required by specialization. Increasingly, the dominant managers are those from the ranks of the administrative staffs, managers of money and numbers, not products and services. Increasingly, their energies are directed toward proper planning and control, rather than risking the uncertainties of plotting uncharted seas. Increasingly, they are focused inward, on holding their territory, on maintaining order. They are now in the business of assuring a predictable return on assets, less and less in the business of building or exploring.

During the 1960s and 1970s most large corporations were in the Administrative or Bureaucratic period. American management had shifted its emphasis from making better products to financial management. Management was based on deductive reasoning alone, supplanting all visionary thinking.

In 1985, Robert H. Hayes of the Harvard Business School argued:

> As corporate staffs have flourished and as the notion of strategy has come to dominate business education and practice, our factories have steadily lost ground to those in other countries where strategy receives far less emphasis and the "professionalization" of management is far less advanced.
>
> Under certain circumstances, the methodology of formal strategic planning and, even worse, the organizational attitudes and relationships that it often cultivates, can impair a company's ability to compete. Moreover, the circumstances under which this occurs is true for much of U.S. industry today.[8]

In this fourth stage of development, the Administrative stage, the company is probably a publicly held corporation, and the investors can get in quick, get out easy, and look for short-term results. The stock analysts play an increasing role in making the company's decisions. Leaps of imagination are hard to explain to outsiders looking for predictable return and steady growth. They want certainty, and certainty can be found by avoiding risks. This priority rules out short-term financial sacrifice that may produce dramatic innovations and a later burst of expansive growth.

Vision and determination create the performance of the future, not trend analysis and projection of past results. To follow trends is not to lead, but to follow—and to follow a mindless and untrustworthy ally at that.

True leadership determines the trends of the future. The wealth of our society comes from those who ignored past trends and determined to create new ones through innovation and dedication. Virtually no entrepreneurial success—Federal Express, Cabbage Patch Dolls, or L. L. Bean—is the result of following trends. They are triumphs of imagination and foresight.

Strategic planners and administrative managers, because they view "the numbers" as more important than knowledge of the product or market, produce plans that assure managers will be extended beyond their field of effective competence.

David K. Hurst, a manager with Russelsteel Inc., provides a vivid account of this phenomenon.[9]

Russelsteel is a Canadian distributor of steel and other industrial products that went public in 1962. It then had five branches and $14 million in sales. The president was the only remaining member of the founding family.

In the early 1960s, the president caught the growth bug. He decided his current second in command, a hard-nosed operations manager, was not the one to manage growth. He hired a Harvard MBA who had spent fifteen years with Procter & Gamble and told him to make the company grow.

Hurst reports that Russelsteel changed after the new manager took over:

> First, it became a good deal more formal, with written policies and plans. Second, a split was created between operating units and the holding entity—a split between managers and investors, between divisions and the head office.
>
> Two groups with distinctly different perspectives began to emerge in the company: the operating managers who ran the profit centers and the "investors," the corporate office heads who ran the holding company on behalf of the public shareholders. This second group acted as a kind of mediating investment group, investing on behalf of the shareholders in a portfolio of divisions.[10]

In other words, the company had turned into a mutual fund. At the same time, the president and executive vice president moved their offices away from the steel operations, symbolic of their new view of themselves as "objective investors."

When senior management becomes detached from the core

operation, they not only become more objective, they become *disinterested*. The temptation to buy something to give their lives more purpose is certain to become overwhelming.

Russelsteel became caught up in the hypnotic dance of acquisition mania, ultimately acquiring twenty-seven separate companies in forty different businesses. Many of the key managers of the acquired companies departed as Russelsteel put its own managers in key positions "to introduce the necessary organization and control." The first four companies Russelsteel bought failed within a few years of acquisition. In one case, the employees of an acquired firm left and with borrowed capital formed their own company. In a few years it had outstripped the acquired business in both size and profitability.

Russelsteel piled acquisition on top of acquisition without digesting and integrating what had been—for the most part—small family-owned businesses. During periods of decline, both in civilizations and companies, it is common for growth to continue, but there is a failure of assimilation. The newly conquered tribes are not becoming citizens, and the lack of social unity retards the progress of all.

The share price of Russelsteel had been holding at about book value through much of the acquisition period, but then began to fall as the failed promise of the grand growth strategy became increasingly evident. Russelsteel's investment activities totally overwhelmed the management of operations and led to the organization's eventual collapse and its own acquisition.

Hurst, after living through this scenario, puts his finger on the problem:

> Now the reader may well feel that these corporate disasters are indicative of management incompetence, faulty analysis, and misdirected strategy. Indeed the proponents of strategic planning usually make this argument. "There is nothing wrong with the model," they say. "All you have to do is apply it properly." Well, there *is* something wrong with the model.[11]

The problem is the fundamental conceptual framework, the understanding of business purpose and the function of management.

The framework assumes that capital is the scarce resource to be rationed among competing investment opportunities. In fact, the current situation in North America is quite the opposite: opportunities are scarce, while capital is plentiful.[12]

The main problem with strategic planning is the assumption that business is about money, rather than about the creation of new products and services, creating new customers and new jobs. This is the real measure of business success. Administrators, once they assume the dominant position, mistakenly believe that business can be reduced to numeric analysis and that predictions can be made in a mechanistic fashion, based on yesterday's performance.

That such thinking has become the culturally accepted norm among today's large organizations is—no matter how sad—predictable. The culture of American business, and perhaps the culture of America in the 1980s, has reached this fourth stage of the life cycle.

HOW TO GET ALONG WITH AN ADMINISTRATOR

If You Work for an Administrator . . .

. . . recognize that he is more likely to reward you for conforming than creating.

. . . understand his essential need for administrative control and discipline. But help him recognize when that control becomes stifling.

. . . recognize who you are and what your ambitions are. If you always work for an Administrator, you will develop the same characteristics. That's fine if you want to be one. If you want to develop into a Synergist, you must gain experience working for Builders and Explorers as well.

If an Administrator Works for You . . .

. . . he is good at taking care of the details. Reward him for that; however, help him to see the larger vision, direction, trends, and reasons why. Keep him in touch with what is important to the business.

. . . the Administrator's systems should serve the business of producing and selling. Help your Administrator see his job as serving those whose performance should be enhanced by his systems, the Builders and Explorers.

THE ORGANIZATION OF THE ADMINISTRATOR

As we have seen, the company is likely to continue to grow during the Administrative phase, but now the growth is of a different order. During the first three stages, new ideas produced new products or services and created new markets. When the railroads were building and expanding, they provided a new service, thereby creating new wealth and new jobs, contributing to the development of society. This is the purpose of business.

But the creation of wealth is a risky business. And, like people, the older and richer institutions become, the less willing they are to take risks. Expansion during the Administrative period is likely to be of a low-risk nature. In this stage, the organization grows by taking the market share from competing companies through cost and price reductions and by the acquisition of other companies serving the same markets.

It is in the Administrative Age that corporations produce the material signs of great success. They build seventy-story glass monuments to themselves. This is when they invest the most in centralized computers. They now have a highly professional class of managers who know more about financial planning, strategy, human resources, and information systems than they do about manufacturing and selling.

To the members of the organization, this stage feels like the healthiest period. They do not sense the decay that has begun. The lack of stress, the absence of urgency, is in itself the danger of this period. The executive who creates or allows such complacency is not earning his keep.

Civilizations experience this state of comfort, too. And when they do, they have ceased their progress, as Toynbee points out:

> The arrested civilizations have achieved so close an adaptation to their environment that they have taken its shape and colour and rhythm instead of impressing the environment with a stamp which is their own. The equilibrium of forces in their life is so exact that all their energies are absorbed in the effort of maintaining the position which they have attained already, and there is no margin of energy left over for reconnoitering the course of the road ahead, or the face of the cliff above them, with a view to a further advance.[13]

The intelligent leader during the Administrative period will realize it is his job to impose a sense of urgency on his organization. He must refocus the company on its customers and competitors.

In the Administrative Age, executives should periodically redesign the entire organization as an antidote to a "condition of ease" by refocusing every manager and employee on his or her customer. Organizational gridlock, and the associated psychological rigidity, will only be stopped by deliberate efforts to enhance cross-functional communication, minimize layers, increase responsibility at the bottom, focus on serving customers, and keeping senior managers in touch with the functional work of the organization.

This design process should be based on the idea of "blowing up" the organization and starting over. The senior management team should formulate a set of principles, objectives, and boundaries defining the culture and structure of the organization. Then teams of employees can design organizational units to conform to those definitions. In the Administrative Age, the staffs and administrative groups will have reached the size where this reassessment is necessary every few years.

The organization passed through the Building and Exploring

Age and is now relatively stable. The compensation system has been estabished. Computers and basic information and accounting systems are in place. There is a performance appraisal system and a system for management development. During the Administrative Age these systems are the focus of much attention, including expensive organizational studies conducted by external and internal consultants. The belief is that higher organizational performance and efficiency can be attained by perfecting these systems. This is the age of belief in systems. While there is merit in improving systems and structure, the belief in their value and importance is misplaced.

The more important an executive believes they are, the more he expects people to conform to systems and structure. This is the age in which large corporations write manuals that define how many square feet each office may be allowed for each pay grade and how many inches the corresponding desk should measure. Such is the stuff of great organizational ritual.

Rituals are forms of control. They make life predictable and orderly. They are useful in all cultures as a means of ordering society and reducing the threat of the troublemakers. Prophets and Barbarians find it extremely difficult, if not impossible, to conform and survive in such an environment. Each year they must submit their annual plans, each quarter their results, each month their objectives. The more rigid the systems and structure, the more creativity is stifled.

To keep order, the leaders increasingly rely on their staff, which gains the strength that comes with nearness to the throne. The Administrator, as the leader of the corporation in this age, has faith in staff specialists. The Builders and Explorers, no longer in control and increasingly separated from the source of power, become increasingly disenchanted. The process becomes self-perpetuating, as powerful staff groups argue for new and increased staff groups and better systems of analysis and controls, all of which serve to increase their scope and influence.

I have been amazed by one CEO of a diversified company clearly in its Administrative Age, who claims to be a great admirer of the lessons in *In Search of Excellence,* who has increased his corporate staff to over eight hundred while cutting engineering, sales, and production personnel across the board. All his subordinate executives wonder whether he and they read the same book.

Your Company Is in the Administrative Age If . . .

. . . much of the energy of the managers is devoted to streamlining and improving procedures.

. . . you are well established in your market and feel confident that customers will continue to buy from you.

. . . there is little sense of urgency or crisis.

. . . your organization is investing in expensive offices and staff headquarters.

. . . new products or services are expected to come from the staff research and development group.

CHALLENGES AND TASKS

Gaining the Competitive Advantage of High Quality and Low Cost When the Administrative stage arrives, the corporation has grown up. The product upon which the original business was built is now mature as well. Earlier, the corporation may have been creating new markets that it could dominate through innovation. Now other competitors have entered the fray, and the battle for market share is fought on the field of cost and quality.

If the Administrators have become dominant, the effort to reduce costs through budgetary control will take precedence over quality improvement. Quality improvement requires a commitment on the part of senior managers to technical excellence and innovation.

American industry during recent years has been plagued by the problem of declining manufacturing competitiveness, which results in poor-quality goods. The emphasis has been overwhelmingly on cost control rather than quality, and managers failed to understand how these goals could be pursued simultaneously. This is easy to understand. By the 1980s most large U.S. corporations had entered their declining stages.

The universities have been unwitting accomplices in the decline. MBAs, upon their entry into the corporation, do not want to serve time in the manufacturing plant. They want to go straight into strategic planning and financial management. Why shouldn't they? Most of their professors spend their time consulting with companies about their strategic planning. Unfortunately, these students want to plan the future of something they do not understand in the first place. They believe that strategic planning and financial management stand on their own, apart from the technical tasks of producing a product or serving a market. This is the great delusion of the Administrator: he believes process is more important than product.

Few senior executives today have run manufacturing operations, few have spent all night in a mill listening to the grinding of machinery and learned to love the people who work the third shift. Steven C. Wheelwright, a Stanford University business professor, explaining the loss of manufacturing competence and jobs in the U.S. semiconductor business, said, "The design engineers in U.S. high-tech companies call all the shots—the manufacturing engineers are second-class citizens, and the manufacturing operations managers are even lower than that."

One of the great challenges of leadership during this fourth stage is to balance the need for creativity and technical competence with financial and planning competence.

If there has been one lesson learned about competitive advantage in recent years, it is that managing quality and costs are interdependent goals. The gap between U.S. and Japanese auto companies proves this.

In the U.S. auto industry, production managers and engineers have unquestionably been under the control of the financial organization. Waves of cost-control programs, cuts, freezes, and reorganizations have swept over General Motors, Ford, and Chrysler.

Toyota, on the other hand, has focused its efforts on quality engineering. The result can be seen in one simple figure: cars produced per employee. In 1986 GM employees produced 11.7 cars;

Toyota, 57.7. The labor cost figure per car reflected the same problem: GM, $4,148; Toyota, $466. And Toyota also placed far ahead of GM in virtually every customer satisfaction and quality survey.

The loss of quality is not just a result of lost technical competence. It also stems from a feeling on the part of those doing the work that they are less and less responsible. Quality, more than anything else, is affected by the commitment of the people with their hands on the product or those who look the customer in the eye. During this fourth stage, as layers of management and control systems are added, the decision making is removed from the first-level employee and supervisor.

Corporations that successfully overcome the doldrums that occur in the Administrative phase encourage and reward both productivity and quality. Quality circles and team management practices, whether among hourly workers or white-collar employees, are a way of stimulating and channeling creative responses. Companies such as Xerox, Milliken & Company, Honda of America, Dun & Bradstreet, and Metropolitan Life are pursuing team management practices that involve every employee in improving production or service. They are getting back to the basic relationship between the individual, his work, and his customer that existed in the earlier days of the corporation when there were fewer external controls and layers of management. Involvement on self-managing teams makes each employee feel both the responsibility of performance and a pride in its achievement.

In the Administrative stage the psychology of commitment is not assured. It must be deliberately managed by designing the structures, systems, management style, and symbols to constantly involve everyone in the improvement process.

Growth Through Acquisition Acquisition strategies can be effective during this period if the culture of the acquired company is integrated into the dominant organization. The purely Administrative manager thinks that he is acquiring an "asset." You don't acquire an asset, you acquire a group of people serving a group of customers, and they, and you, must learn to work together.

The Dun & Bradstreet Corporation, with more than thirty divisions, has grown largely through acquisition, and there is—as Jack Murray discovered—a common language, common tools and techniques, and opportunities for synergy.

Murray's Plan Services, Inc., a provider of administration and claims handling for group insurance companies, was bought by Dun & Bradstreet when it was still an entrepreneurial, rapidly growing venture. Murray is now a vice president of D&B. As a Prophet and Barbarian by habit, this once entrepreneur and now executive of a multidivision corporation, is appreciated. He is still likely to burst forth with ideas and initiatives. Both his and his company's personalities have been successfully integrated within the 120-year-old Dun & Bradstreet.

Continental Can Company did not fare as well. Continental Can was a dominant container manufacturer with cash to expand. As Administrators became dominant in the corporation, it lost its creativity and turned to acquisitions. Unfortunately it did not understand the principle of cultural integration. Indeed, it fell victim to the classic portfolio management madness. It acquired insurance, forest products, and oil and gas businesses. The name was changed to The Continental Group. As in so many cases, the sum of these various businesses equaled less than the value of their parts. The result: Continental was acquired; the insurance, forest products, and oil and gas businesses were sold off, and now only the sound and steady profit makers, the can and container manufacturing operation, remain. Tremendous energy and resources were spent going around in a circle.

Peter Drucker has prescribed five rules for successful acquisitions. All imply the ability to integrate the business and culture of the acquired with that of acquirer.

1. An acquisition will succeed only if the acquiring company thinks through what it can contribute to the business it is buying, not what the acquired company can contribute to the acquirer, no matter how attractive the expected "synergy" may look.

2. Successful diversification by acquisition, like all

successful diversification, requires a common core of unity. The two businesses must have in common either markets or technology. . . . Without such a core of unity, diversification, especially by acquisition, never works; financial ties alone are insufficient.

3. No acquisition works unless the people in the acquiring company respect the product, the markets, and the customers of the company they acquire. The acquisition must be a "temperamental fit."

4. Within a year or so, the acquiring company must be able to provide top management for the company it acquires [in case the acquired managers decide to defect]. It is an elementary fallacy to believe one can "buy" management.

5. Within the first year of a merger, it is important that a large number of people in the management groups of both companies receive substantial promotions across the lines—that is, from one of the former companies to the other. The goal is to convince managers in both companies that the merger offers them personal opportunities.[14]

It is sound judgment to acquire businesses that can be intelligently integrated in a manner that both stimulates the existing managers with diversity of thought and experience and provides for genuine technology transfer that may add innovation. For example, Southwestern Bell acquired Metromedia, Inc. Their cellular phone business is clearly related to the primary business of Southwestern Bell and represents an opportunity to utilize present resources in a compatible enterprise. On the other hand, NYNEX acquired eighty-three IBM Product Centers, retail computer and electronic stores from which IBM couldn't squeeze a decent return. Is a New York–based telephone company, with managers trained and conditioned by a lifetime in a highly regulated business, likely to make a small computer store profitable? The chance of its beating Computerland or Tandy Corporation's Radio Shack seems remote indeed. If the same dollars required to buy the product centers had been returned to NYNEX shareholders in the form of dividends, I am quite certain those investors would gain a higher return by making their own investment decisions.

The process of acquiring disparate business assures the alienation of senior managers. These managers begin to see themselves as superior to, and increasingly disinterested in, the primary business.

Civilizations start to decline when social integration stops and when the leaders become alienated from their followers. The same is true in corporations.

The Challenge to Stimulate Creativity Many corporate leaders fail to understand that the real business of the corporation is innovation. In today's rapidly changing, highly competitive business environment, the corporation must constantly reinvent itself—its products, services, and marketing—in order to grow. Earlier we recognized that the corporation at this point in its life cycle must respond to internal challenges. The challenges of creating new products, services, and marketing methods—as well as controlling costs and quality—are all internal ones.

These challenges require creativity. But unfortunately, at this time in the corporation's life, the culture is less and less supportive of creative responses. Creative responses are always, by definition, *different*. The people who develop them usually are out of place in the Administrative Age. The Administrator will want to manage creativity by assigning it to a specific department and giving it a budget. How much money will be allocated to research and development, and what will be the return on that investment? the Administrator will ask, thinking that he is working on a solution to the "creativity problem." He is using his rational faculties to solve a nonrational problem. His approach to the problem *is* the problem.

The task is to build a total culture that supports creativity. It must not only tolerate a degree of disorder, but foment an atmosphere of adolescent enthusiasm. This culture is not the most comfortable for the Administrator. It is a culture in which everything does not have to be counted and recorded because the emphasis is not on control, but on achieving victories.

In the Administrative Age, rewards for creativity are "well managed" and equitable, probably in the range of 3 percent to 10 percent of annual compensation, insignificant compared with what may be expected by the entrepreneur, who takes his ideas outside the corporation. The highly creative individual who is likely to invent the new product thrives in an environment of crisis, high reward, and low control; he wants to feel an intimate part of the risk/reward game. For this reason the temptation to start his own business and experience the ultimate in entrepreneurship pulls hard at the strings of creative talent. The large corporation must compete for creative talent with a larger culture in which capital is the cheap commodity and creative talent and energy the more precious ingredient.

The Beginning of Corporate Socialism and the Midlife Crisis The use and distribution of capital changes in this fourth stage. During earlier stages, stockholders had higher expectations for capital appreciation and lower expectations for dividend returns. Now the company is more profitable, asset growth will be slower, and the stockholders will expect higher dividends. Corporate management, however, will begin a policy of deliberately managing stockholder expectations. They will pay out far lower dividends than they could. Holding capital within the organization for managers to invest in acquisitions, rather than paying it out in dividends for its rightful owners to invest, will gradually become a habitual strategy. If the money is lost, the managers do not feel the pain; it is the stockholders who have no say in the acquisition decisions who lose. This strategy will begin to alienate stockholders and eventually drive down the price of the stock. The managers themselves, now a professional class, own less of the stock of the corporation than earlier managers, causing them to have little interest in maximizing dividends.

Management has developed a view of its own prerogatives that prevents the distribution of profits to stockholders. They won't admit it, but they view stockholders as distant, disinterested and unworthy of receiving high dividends. They are making a value judgment that will eventually cause rebellion in the Aristocratic stage. The Administrators now believe the stockholders will be satisfied with dividends similar to those paid in the past, despite the now high profits.

The Administrative Age begins the period of *corporate socialism,* which springs from the arrogant assumption by executives, and their board of directors, that they have the sole right to decide how the stockholders' profits should be used. Managers certainly should reinvest in the business to further the interests of *that* business. But when they begin to diversify into totally unrelated businesses—as is typical of this stage—they take on the role of a bank or mutual fund.

The diversification into unrelated businesses is a direct consequence of social fragmentation. The board of directors is another fragmented social class. They are hired professionals. Often they are not owners of the corporation and so do not share the desire for return on the shareholders' investment. They are, therefore, quite willing to allow administrators to spend stockholders' money on investments they know nothing about.

This loss of dedication and shift to a mutual fund strategy creates a spiral of lost competence. Administrators are now not as fearful of being bested in their core business. If they fail, it will be masked by the revenues and profits from the other businesses. And the more they diversify, the less they need to maintain competence in their core business. The loss of that competence is now almost guaranteed.

Such corporate practices create the same malaise as political socialism. Supposedly objective state planners, not dedicated to any particular activity, make decisions about capital allocation. The lack of personal attachment results in the absence of a fear of failure. Without the fear of failure, dedication soon falls off. The same thing happens during the Administrative Age of the corporation. Administrators are not wedded to one particular business, and the more diversified the company becomes, the less interested the Administrator is in any particular line.

I have come to believe that there is a factor governing corporate diversification that is extremely simple. It is what I will call the "tedium trap." Surprisingly, senior executives are like the rest of us. They become bored, tired of the repetition and routine of it all.

By the time a manager has worked his way up to president or chairman of the board, he is anxious to explore new territory. He yearns for a change.

This is the midlife crisis, when middle-aged men feel obsessed with finding something new. There is a wonderful attraction to novelty, change for change's sake. To engage in new business is to feel young again. And when one cannot create that within, one looks for something to acquire, a new woman, Porsche, boat, or corporate acquisition. Much of the diversified acquisition that takes place in American corporations occurs for the simple reason that the senior executives want new challenges. I seriously doubt that you will find one executive who will admit it, but they are simply trying to escape the tedium trap.

Building Customer-Focused Administration Among the new internal challenges is building efficient administration that does not become detached from the primary business purpose. The best way to accomplish this is to build into staff management the principle of *customer focus.*

Just as sales, marketing, and production managers do their jobs most effectively when they have a clear sense of responsibility to, and communication with, the customer, so must the administrative staff keep a clear orientation toward their customer. Their customer, however, is within: the manufacturing department, the sales organization, senior management, and so on.

Executives should ask each staff group to specifically define their customers and explain how they will listen and respond to their needs. Just as marketing and manufacturing should conduct regular surveys, focus groups, and other forms of customer feedback, the groups should do exactly the same. Some companies, such as 3M, have gone so far as to have line organizations purchase the services of inside staff groups, giving them the option of buying outside services rather than spending their funds on internal staff groups if the price is not competitive. This practice causes the staff groups to be more responsive.

Problems develop in this stage when the staff groups (such as finance, personnel, and planning) develop a closer working relationship with the senior executive than the senior line manager (operations and sales). The chief executive may then rely more on the senior staff and less on the operating managers, who become alienated. The result affects the entire organization. A similar situation developed when President Reagan's National Security Counsel staff became the "inner circle," and their advice was given more weight than the senior operating managers, the secretaries of the State and Defense departments. Those officers with responsibility for implementation of policy and with the best network of informed and experienced personnel came to be ignored in favor of the close-at-hand NSC staff. The Iran arms sale fiasco was a direct result of this misalignment of staff and line managers.

◆

The Bureaucrat

The Tight Grip of Control

The piper who has lost his cunning can no longer conjure the feet of the multitude into a dance; and if, in rage and panic, he now attempts to turn himself into a drill sergeant or a slave-driver, and to coerce by physical force a people whom he feels that he can no longer lead by his old magnetic charm, then, all the more surely and more swiftly, he defeats his own intention; for the followers who had merely flagged and fallen behind as the heavenly music died away will be stung by a touch of the whip into active rebellion.

—ARNOLD TOYNBEE

The primary characteristic of the Bureaucratic Age is a loss of social purpose resulting in a loss of unity. The layered classes of the structure fail to understand each other and are increasingly devoted to their own self-interests. The leaders divorce themselves from their followers. The work force proceeds to develop its own bureaucracy to protect it from unresponsive leadership. The fabric begins to rip.

With the Bureaucratic Age comes the age of skepticism. The employees in the Bureaucratic organization begin to doubt their leaders have a clear vision of the organization's future. They begin to doubt the value of dedicating their career to the company. The

110

managers are beginning to doubt their own strategies. The leaders are beginning to lose faith in the primary business. They seek salvation in a mirage of unfamiliar enterprises. They do not yet understand that the problem is not with the business, but with themselves.

Research shows that retired persons who have lost purpose deteriorate both mentally and physically. The Bureaucrat corporation is in the process of losing its purpose and health.

In the Bureaucratic Age the members of the organization spend their declining energies not on customers or competition, but on the struggle within. The more they focus on internal discord, the less they are capable of responding creatively to the challenges of the external environment. Instead, they enter into mergers and acquisitions, which increase the weight of the uncreative mass while reducing the number of creative leaders.

THE CHARACTER OF THE BUREAUCRAT

When we think of a bureaucrat, we are most likely to think of the slow-moving passive government bureaucrat, the obstacle to action. But there is another, equally dangerous kind, the aggressive bureaucrat who spins a tight web of control that initially squeezes cost savings and efficiencies from an organization but soon after also squeezes out the creative talent, resulting in an organization incapable of generating new wealth.

The passive bureaucrat, usually found in staff jobs or government agencies, is less dangerous because he is inactive and merely slows the progress of others. The aggressive bureaucrat is more dangerous because his initial success—often through cost cutting—allows him to build an empire. That his empire is merely a conglomeration of the past creative work of others, and represents a net loss in wealth-producing capability, does not deter him.

The British Empire was successful largely because of the competence of its administrators, the British civil servants. Regardless of one's judgment of colonization, any fair examination of British rule in India, for example, would conclude the British administrators maintained the order of the realm efficiently. England ran its colony with 1,299 members of the Indian Civil Service, who were essentially the entire central government of the time. Today, the Indian central government employs 3.3 million persons. During the colonial period the civil service could be accused of failing to *encourage* development. Today the civil service is widely recognized for *suppressing* development. That is not surprising. Generally, the greater the administrative control, the weaker the tendency toward development and expansion.

A century ago, in order to control production in India, England introduced the practice of requiring industrial companies to obtain licenses. The practice did not end with the departure of the British administrators. Today, before an individual can engage in any industrial development project, he will probably have to wait for up to two years for eight different committees to approve his request. Until recently an industrial investment of $16 million or more required cabinet approval. The habit of control, copied from the British, so inhibits Indian industry that the government-run steel authority produces steel at about twice the world price and with about 30 percent more employees than the world average.

Bureaucracy is not merely numbers of people, committees, and review meetings. It is a system of values, with its own rewards that impels its members to perpetuate those controls. As one member of the Indian bureaucracy admitted recently, "I don't have money, I don't have intellectual power, but what I can do is keep J.R.D. Tata [a leading Indian industrialist] waiting outside my office for twenty minutes."[1]

In the corporation, the board of directors is now made up of those who are indebted to management. They provide input and feedback that conforms to, rather than challenges, the views of management. Many board members have never even visited a manufacturing plant or witnessed the selling process. They neither know nor care about them. They care about the stock price, debt to equity ratios, and other results of past creativity that will ultimately worsen due to the neglect of the productive work of the business. The board members are spectators who enter the stadium after the game is over, stare at the scoreboard, and mumble approval of the coach's strategy. Most of these spectators wouldn't know a well-executed play if they saw one.

The decline and its cause can easily be seen by contrasting management behavior at General Motors and Honda. At General Motors senior executives are driven to work by a chauffeur, their cars kept in heated garages and tended by company mechanics. This all but guarantees that the executive remains out of touch with the workings of his own product.

Senior Honda managers all drive their own cars, made in their own plant, to work. While GM is investing billions of dollars in automation to reduce the human factor in production, Honda is insisting that a manager cannot make a decision, or solve a problem, unless he is "on the spot." While all senior GM managers are in isolated office buildings, the president of Honda of America is sitting in an open office area, with all of the other managers at the Marysville, Ohio, auto plant, helping to design a new engine. The difference has nothing to do with Japanese versus American management. It is entirely a function of life cycle position.

Leaders in this fifth stage of the life cycle begin to devote themselves to the symbols of their authority rather than the substance of their products and services. They build taller buildings, have larger and more grandiose offices, because these symbols talk to them. The symbols say "You are in charge. You do know what you're doing. You are an effective leader."

The annual report to the stockholders will have on its cover not the new factory or research lab, but a photograph of the new office building. And the recipients of that report will fail to understand that the higher the building, the more people are employed, not in the production of profits, but in reporting on the work of others, planning the work of others, and spending the money of others—the others in this case being the shareholders who have received the report.

The mosques of Islam became most ornate and expansive when the expansion of the faith came to an end. The Pyramids of Egypt became the obsession of the pharaohs as they became progressively divorced from their subjects and convinced that they were the gods themselves. And the Pan Am Building and the Sears Tower were built, like so many others, during the period when the corporation was losing its vitality and the character and priorities of the leaders were shifting from substance to symbols.

You May Be a Bureaucrat If . . .

. . . you spend most of your time in meetings reviewing what has already happened or should have happened.

. . . you cannot remember when you last participated in the development of a new product or service . . . and you don't think that's your job.

. . . you are more concerned with how you and your company are viewed by Wall Street analysts than by your customers.

. . . you believe tighter control will solve many of your organization's problems.

. . . you spend more time with central staff managers than with line sales and production managers.

THE BUREAUCRAT IN HISTORY

Comrades, we are building not a land of idlers where rivers flow with milk and honey but the most organized and most industrious society in human history. And the people living in that society will be the most industrious, conscientious, organized, and politically conscious in history.
—LEONID BREZHNEV, 1972

As long as the bosses pretend they are paying us a decent wage, we will pretend that we are working.
—COMMON SAYING AMONG SOVIET WORKERS,
ABOUT THE SAME DATE

The decline of a corporation is often explained by pointing to external events such as competition, technology, changing economic or market conditions. Similarly, some historians have explained the decline of a civilization by pointing to changes in the physical environment such as earthquake, volcanic eruption, or plague, limits on physical expansion, or the attack of external competitors. Arnold Toynbee examined each of these and rejected all external explanations, leaving only the internal cause, the loss of human vitality. Toynbee's analysis is based on his evaluation of the fall of twenty-one major civilizations, a huge database of cultural decline. It is worth reviewing his arguments.

The Romans, great builders of roads, irrigation systems, and other means of conquering the physical environment, began to lose that control beginning in the fifth century. The Roman roads fell into disrepair. But this was not from any retardation in the technical or administrative skills required for road building. It was the result of social decay within. The citizens of Rome were increasingly spending their funds on leisure and luxury, unwilling to pay additional taxes for the general welfare. Roads, taken for granted, were no longer a challenge that excited public concern.

Similarly, the decay of the roads in and around New York City in recent years is not the result of an increasing severity of the physical environment, or a failure of technical skill, but a failure of commitment. And may it not also be true that the loss of the ability to make high-quality automobiles that appeal to Americans was also caused by a failure of social health and vitality? In history, as well as in the corporation, the failure will always appear to have a technical, physical, or material root. Yet despite appearances, it is a condition of ease that dulls human energies.

A second possible cause of decay that Toynbee rejected is the civilization's inability to expand geographically. On the contrary, it appears that geographic expansion, particularly of a violent nature, tends to occur at the very time of social disintegration within. The Roman Empire was expanding into the British Isles and Scotland while Roman society was dissolving. The leaders of the society may make a frantic effort to appear in control, to maintain their strong and youthful appearance, by engaging in particularly dramatic expansions.

Similarly, large and wealthy corporations that have lost their ability to create new enterprises within—and are increasingly hindered by internal discord—may turn outward, buying other companies in an attempt to appear vital and healthy. In reality this is itself a sign of an inner cancer. The acquisition of Reliance Electric by Exxon is just one example.

A third possible explanation for the defeat of a civilization is that it suffers at the hands of attack from alien barbarians. However, Toynbee points to many examples of attack from alien forces—the attack by Muslims on Christiandom and the attack of the Mongols on Japan, for example—demonstrating that such attacks may prove a stimulant rather than a source of defeat. In all cases where alien attack has proved fatal, the society was already in an advanced state of social decline and was unable to muster any effective response to the external challenge.

For a civilization and a company, there is always external competition. Edward Gibbon in his *Decline and Fall of the Roman Empire* writes of the fall of Rome:

> The mortal blow was delivered at least 600 years earlier, and the hand that dealt it was the victim's own. We are still confronted with the question why the victim was overtaken by a suicidal mania of this kind at this time . . . we have arrived at the conclusion that the verdict must be one of suicide and not murder.[2]

Toynbee concluded that the only remaining explanation for why civilizations fail is the failure of the society to respond to challenge, the failure of self-determination. Most other historians agree. H. G. Wells wrote:

> The two centuries of order between 27 B.C. and 180 A.D. may be counted as among the wasted opportunities of mankind. It was an age of spending rather than of creation, an age of architecture and trade in which the rich grew richer and the poor poorer and the soul and spirit of man decayed.[3]

> The Roman Imperial system . . . at its best had a bureaucratic administration which kept the peace of the

world for a time and failed altogether to secure it. . . . The clue to all its failure lies in the absence of any free mental activity and any organization for the increase, development, and application of knowledge. It respected wealth and it despised science. . . . It was a colossally ignorant and unimaginative empire. It foresaw nothing.[4]

The defeat is a failure of creative leadership, but the leaders—of either civilization or corporation—are as much victims as they are oppressors. Because of the numbers of layers below them, the information they receive is increasingly inaccurate and distorted. Because of the weight of the potential power they wield, their subordinates are less and less likely to confront them with the truth. This physical, intellectual, and spiritual separation between the leaders and the led is growing. And with that growth, the ability of the society to determine its own future is gradually being swept away.

This failure of leadership has been repeated in each of the deceased civilizations.

We have also described the nature of these breakdowns in non-material terms as a loss of creative power in the souls of the creative individuals, or the creative minorities, who have been the leaders of any given civilization at any given stage in the history of its growth; and we have seen that this failure of vitality on the leaders' side divests them of their magic power to influence and attract the uncreative masses.[5]

When it comes to bureaucracy, we in the United States are more than one Sputnik behind the Russians. We are rank amateurs.

Mikhail Gorbachev has set out to free the energies of the Russian people from the chains of their own rigid bureaucracy. The constipation of commerce, so firmly cemented by the systems and structure of the Soviet Union, are the strongest weapons against its own expansion and prosperity.

The culture of present-day Russia has followed the life cycle curve without significant deviation. Marx and Lenin were the Prophets of the Soviet system and are viewed with the same reverence as religious Prophets in other societies. They were the men of ideas, with Lenin transitioning into the Barbarian leadership period. Like other Prophets, they had little concern with the immediate; their eye was firmly fixed on a long-term vision. Stalin was pure Barbarian, with an undeniable case of dementia that has afflicted most Barbarian leaders whose power remained unchecked. While many Builders and Explorers among the ranks carried out their assignments, none rose to dominance. When absolute Barbarians stay in power too long, their personal characteristics tend to become transmitted into the systems and structure, creating the most absolute form of bureaucracy.

Bureaucrats place great emphasis on plans and planning. The Soviets, like our large corporations, have invested much in strategic planning. Hedrick Smith, *New York Times* correspondent, who served in Moscow for many years and provides one of the most complete documentaries of Soviet life in his book *The Russians*, describes the cultural phenomena:

> The Plan is proffered by Soviet Marxists as the key to scientific management of manpower and resources, the unerring lever for achieving maximum growth and rising productivity, the Utopian device for assuring the coordinated functioning of the world's second mightiest economy. The Plan comes close to being the fundamental law of the land. "Fulfill the Plan" is one of the most incessant incantations of Soviet life. Publicly, the Plan is treated with almost mystical veneration, as if endowed with some superhuman faculty for raising mortal endeavor to a higher plane, freed of human foibles.[6]

Bureaucrats, whether in the Soviet government or the American corporation, have an almost religious belief in the power of plans to achieve goals. In either setting they have about equal effect.

It can be argued that the early Five Year Plans of Stalin served a useful function, coordinating scarce resources, focusing energy and materials on logical priorities. Plans *can* be useful. But like all administrative methods, they fail to address the substance of the matter. They do not stimulate the flow of creative ideas. They do not produce an innovative microchip, the automotive engineering of BMW, or the dedicated spirit of the family farmer. Scientific management is offered up with the same religious zeal by virtually all bureaucracies; the nature of that science (a misnomer in every case!) varies with the culture, but the effect is always the same: tighter control, centralization of authority, and decline of creativity and dedication.

The more bureaucratic the society, the more distinct the division between the controlled and the controllers. Democracy is virtually impossible when control mechanisms are relied upon to achieve economic performance. Democracy requires leaders closely in touch with their followers. Reliance on control divorces leaders and followers. There is no better example of this than the tendency (despite the communist vision) toward class distinctions within the Soviet Union. Defector Arkady N. Shevchenko, a former ambassador at the United Nations, described his own training.

> Our professors tried to hammer into us the idea that Soviet society was ruled by the working class, the so-called dictatorship of the proletariat, the basic Marxist-Leninist concept for the transitional period from capitalism to socialism. But the proletariat was (and is) in fact despised by the elite, except for a few designated by the Party as "heroes of the Socialist labor" and used for propaganda purposes.[7]

Another corollary to the rule of bureaucracy is an entrenched resistance to change. The more the leading class becomes distinct, the more invested it becomes in its systems and structure, and the greater the resistance to change. To change the Soviet system Mikhail Gorbachev will have to curb drastically the power of the *nomenklatura* class that controls Soviet life. Arkady Shevchenko, himself a product of this class, is certain the bureaucracy will prevail.

He [Gorbachev] is a product of the Soviet system, or to be precise, of the Party apparatus. One would be absolutely wrong to entertain the idea that he would want to alter substantially the existing system . . . changes in Moscow's top leadership have had a rather marginal effect on the essential character of the Kremlin's power structure and on its policy direction. . . . It seems to me very doubtful that the *nomenklatura* class will disappear any time soon under the coming generations of Kremlin leaders.[8]

Can the Russians reform simply because there is a better way of achieving productive effort? Is our own Congress capable of reforming its budgeting process, which obviously fails to serve the people well? Is our government capable of reforming the judicial and penal systems, which every observer has concluded increases rather than decreases the probability of further crime? The history of the decline of civilizations and institutions would answer, No!

The explanation is simple. Reform requires great sacrifice and effort. In the absence of competition, or internal revolution, the dominant class does not experience sufficient pressure to force them to the expense of reform.

It is unfortunate that the more entrenched the bureaucracy, the lower the probability of peaceful change. It is the unequal distribution of power, the absence of checks and balances, that is the antecedent to revolution. When the alienation is complete, the leaders ascend to the state of aristocracy, and the subjects have no alternative but open revolt or defection.

THE BUSINESS BUREAUCRAT

Harold Geneen, former CEO of ITT, was the supreme aggressive Bureaucrat. No manager was ever more dedicated to the discipline of financial control, management by the numbers. Geneen had no love for any product, customer, or technology. It was not important what business he was in. He believed in the numbers and the systems to drive the numbers. He created structures well suited to this relentless pursuit of financial control. And he achieved that control. But simultaneously he drove out any impulse toward creativity.

He made numerous acquisitions, but he failed to integrate disparate cultures. He failed to understand the limitations of control. And in his failure he proved that business is not a business of numbers alone.

In 1950 Jones & Laughlin Steel, recognizing their need for administrative controls, hired Harold Geneen away from Bell & Howell to create a system of financial management. J&L was a classic example of a company that had been dominated by Builders and Explorers who never learned to appreciate the need for administration. The entire steel industry was in much the same shape. Geneen found that the operating managers at J&L had no notion of costs, no concept of return on investment, the value of inventory, or the cost of materials. The greatest financial goal of J&L operating managers was to obtain the largest-possible slice of the annual capital appropriations. And with no accountability for return on investment, why not? Operating managers ignored the "bean counters."

Prior to Geneen, the "bean counters" were viewed as subservient clerks who had no say in decision making. But Geneen was an accountant of a different color. He was an Administrator painted with the personality of the Barbarian. He would change the relationship between accounting and line managers forever, not only at J&L, but throughout much of American industry.

The story of Harold Geneen and the dominance of numbers-oriented management, central staff, and conglomeration is the story of administration gone mad. The growing dominance of financial managers, and the lawyers who follow closely behind, coincides directly with the decline of American competitiveness.

At J&L Steel, Geneen, with messianic zeal, built an accounting department with a vision of remaking the company according to the gospel of financial control.

> Geneen's people pried a complete description of J&L's
> product line out of sales and approximate costs for each
> item from operations. The operations people were not

deliberately balky. They honestly did not know their exact costs for any product or production level. No one had ever suggested that such knowledge could affect the cost of steel. Costs are costs, aren't they? No, Geneen said, they are variable; and to know how they vary with production is the key to their control. Besides, knowing exact costs for every product allows a measurement of performance. It solves the problem of comparing last month's oranges with this month's apples.[9]

Geneen and his people developed the mill operating cost control program (MOCC), a standard operating cost program that changed the way the steel company was managed. Suddenly mill managers were held accountable for each cost item.

Now the managers' monthly review letters bloomed from a couple of pages to half-inch books crammed with performance statistics. Managers appeared at the monthly meeting flanked by their accountants (instantly upgraded) and sales and operating people. They had to answer for each variance from the budget, explain each deviation from standard. Whatever the cause, the MOCC alerted management to trouble and pointed to the probable villain.[10]

Harold Geneen, company controller, sat at the side of the president during monthly review meetings and didn't hesitate to fire questions at the once dominant sales and production managers. Discovering that one product produced higher profits, he would demand to know why the salesmen were not pushing that line.

Sales managers were not used to being instructed by an accountant. They hated it! Sales and production had always run the company, barely tolerating accountants. And now this humiliation. As John Timberlake, vice president of sales, blurted out, "I don't need any shiny-ass clerk to tell me how to run my business!"

Timberlake was a steel man. Steel had been his livelihood—and his life—for fifty years. The steel produced by each of the major steel companies was essentially the same product, a commodity, sold on price. The primary factor in marketing success was personal relationships, service, rapport between the members of the fraternity of buyers and sellers. Geneen was an intruder in this world—an intruder who understood his numbers but not those that produced sales or steel. "Steel was no more in Geneen's blood than any other industry had been or would be. He would never be a steel man or any sort of industry man. He was always a return-on-investment man, a pennies-per-share man."[11]

Initially Geneen's system was successful in improving return on investment. There was no doubt that not only J&L but most of the steel industry was in desperate need of more systematic financial controls. The industry adopted the cost control approach to steel production. Increasingly the dominant managers were not steel men, but finance men. If the short-term improvement in steel profits can be attributed to Geneen's system, it is only fair to ask, what about the long-term loss? Is there a relationship between the replacement of men who loved steel with men who loved numbers and the decline of the industry? If both groups had worked together in synergy—combining the technical product competence of the Builder and Explorer with the efficiency and control of a competent Administrator, the steel industry might have remained more competitive.

After a stay as executive vice president at Raytheon, Geneen became chief executive of ITT, where he had complete freedom to implement management according to Geneen. Immediately he brought in consultants and others upon whom he could rely to help him develop the structures and systems of control. That which he could not control he did not want. During his first years he sold the 22 percent of NEC (Nippon Electric Company) that was held by ITT. He sold ITT's holdings in the Swedish telephone company L. M. Ericsson because they would not submit to his demands for full disclosure of all of their numbers. By any fair analysis those two properties today, had he retained them, would be worth more than all of the combined acquisitions of ITT.

The aspect of Geneen's systems that was most infuriating to ITT managers was having local financial controllers reporting directly to the corporate staff rather than to local business unit managers. The idea was that these financial managers were to remain as objective consultants, working with their unit managers, but be free to report with absolute honesty to headquarters. This sounded good. In reality, human nature intervened. Financial managers were not part of the local management team, but "outsiders," "spies," with the power to bring inquisitorial visits of the corporate staff.

The company became dominated by Geneen's corporate staff.

> Staff played two roles for Geneen. First, they were his eyes and ears on the line. He fostered the traditional adversarial wariness between staff and line with a policy that one former staff man calls "dynamic tension." Others called it spying. Geneen chose, the staffer says, "to build conflict into the organization, to make sure all the big problems would bubble up to him, so he could preserve for himself the option of being involved in the decisions. That was true at the highest levels. . . . Staff had unquestioned access to every unit, were included in everything, had to review nearly every step of every plan, process, and new product and that was with no problems in sight. . . . The second function of staff was to sniff out problems." [12]

ITT entered into a long period of buying and selling corporate properties. Many came and went. Avis, Sheraton Hotels, Jabsco Pump, Bobbs-Merrill, Airport Parking Company of America, Modern Life Insurance, Hamilton Life, and so on. From 1965 through 1967 Geneen made forty acquisitions. [13] Each year the company reported larger revenues and larger profits. It looked great. Geneen and his system were on a roll. The idea of growth through acquisition took on greater momentum throughout American industry as a result of Geneen's apparent success. But there was no social glue, no common bond of dedication to any field, industry, or market.

One of ITT's acquisitions was LSI, and its trauma points out the problems that began to develop in many of the acquired businesses. Bill Levitt was the Prophet/Barbarian who revolutionized home building. He was responsible for the famed Levittown. Bill Levitt developed on-site production-line methods for home construction that provided single-family housing at an economical price.

The housing business is one of intuition and wheeling and dealing, buying properties in the field from farmers on a hunch and guessing at the price of what homes in the neighborhood would sell for.

In housing development there was no predictable revenue stream. Unlike the ITT telephone equipment business with a dependent client base, once a house was sold, you started all over again. Every year you had to create new properties and new clients.

Geneen was warned that this was a business ITT should not be in, but investment banker Felix Rohatyn convinced Geneen that LSI had reduced the housing business to a basic manufacturing enterprise, not unlike other ITT businesses. Some suspect that Bill Levitt knew that his business had peaked before the ITT purchase.

Soon after the acquisition Levitt was replaced by Dick Wasserman, considered one of the best pure managers at ITT. Wasserman brought into LSI an excellent team. The problem was that they were expected to grow a business they did not understand. So to meet the expectations for growth, they soon began to acquire other companies.

LSI bought United Homes Corporation, a Seattle builder, immediately before the collapse of the housing market caused by the decline of Boeing. United's sales dropped from $33 million in 1969 to $5 million in 1972. The former owner admitted he would have been bankrupt had he been unable to unload the business. LSI then went into apartments and condominiums just in time for a market glut there. They then opened a mobile home factory, perfectly timed to the contraction of that business.

Wasserman was expected to produce growth at LSI, and he was trying to do it the Geneen way. Look at the numbers. The statistics show a period of years of upward growth trend. The statistics don't lie, do they? Buy!

But statistics do lie! They don't always tell the whole story. The only thing certain about a trend line is that it will reverse itself. It is only a matter of time. To predict the turnaround you must know the substance of the business. You must be dedicated to the product and market. Neither Wasserman nor Geneen knew or were dedicated to the housing business.

In 1972 LSI lost $600,000. In 1973 it lost $28 million. Through 1975 the total loss was more than $100 million. One estimate put it at over $230 million.

The conduct of business is a process of communication. If you are in the aerospace engineering business, there is a language symbolic of that culture. If you are in the arts, banking, or building, the same is true. One of the problems at ITT and other conglomerates was that communication became babble. Managers did not understand each other. Yes, they spoke the same language (Geneen insisted that all his European managers speak English; he even conducted European meetings on New York time), but they did not understand the meaning behind the words. Employee relations, inventory turns, efficiency, and planning are all bound to the context of the business. Each business has its own culture, symbolized by the language and the meaning behind the language. It is difficult enough to master the complex significance of language in one business. To interpret across dozens of unrelated businesses is virtually impossible.

The downfall of Geneen and ITT was a failure of integration, a failure of social unity. When Rome was expanding in its early days, the conquered people became Roman citizens. They were culturally integrated. They learned to speak the same language. Later, the conquered did not become citizens, they were not socially integrated. The alienation of leaders and led began. The culture declined.

The measure of a successful acquisition is whether the combined value is greater than the value of the parts alone. Conglomerates in general, and ITT in particular, have failed this test. It is this failure that drives corporations such as Exxon and ITT to return to the business they know.

Diversification has proven so bad a business for ITT that, according to one analyst, nearly all the profits reported by the giant in the first three quarters of 1984 existed only on paper; its assets, estimated *Business Week*, were selling at maybe half their breakup value; the dividend had been cut; and in the wake of that last trauma, a financier was preparing a raid on the wreck. ITT's latest CEO, Rand V. Araskog, had cut the dividend to finance the investment badly needed, and shamefully overdue, to restore ITT's strength in its base market, U.S. telecommunications. But, of course, the entire rationale of conglomeration was to enhance the financial strength of the whole by combining its parts. In ITT's case, the original Geneen strategy had plainly had the reverse effect.[14]

HOW TO GET ALONG WITH A BUREAUCRAT

If You Work for a Bureaucrat . . .

. . . he will tend to focus on performance that fits the system, without asking whether it is the right performance. Help him by asking him questions that will lead him to consider the "why" questions that may lead to more creative responses.

. . . the Bureaucrat needs order and conformity. Nonconformity makes him anxious. Don't be weird. It's hell to work for a nervous boss, particularly if you're the one who's making him nervous.

. . . you need to serve as a buffer for your subordinates. You must manage them to produce creative responses without interference from your Bureaucratic boss. Don't make your problem your subordinates' problem.

If a Bureaucrat Works for You . . .

. . . he better be in a staff and not a line job.

. . . you need to control him to make sure that he does not work his web of stifling systems and structure around others.

. . . he will constantly be complaining about others who are violating the sanctity of his systems. Learn to say, "So what?"

. . . reward him for developing and managing the most efficient administrative processes. Define efficient as with the fewest-possible staff, requiring the least time of line managers.

THE ORGANIZATION OF THE BUREAUCRAT

Centralization at the national capital or within a business undertaking always glorifies the importance of pieces of paper. This dims the sense of reality. As men and organizations acquire a preoccupation with papers, they become less understanding, less perceptive of the reality of those matters with which they should be dealing. Making decisions from paper has a dehumanizing effect. Much of man's inhumanity to man is explained by it. Almost all great observers of mankind have noted it.

—DAVID E. LILIENTHAL

The Bureaucratic organization is one consumed by love of its own physical form. The process of specialization has evolved now to the point where there are subgroups of subgroups, each performing disjointed studies, evaluations, and plans, few of which will have any effect.

The Bureaucrat will constantly reorganize, searching for the structural solution to the spiritual problem. These frequent changes in organization will produce employees who will constantly be wondering if they will have a job once the latest reorganization is finished. In the developing stages, employees looked to the future with high expectations. In the declining organization, employees look to the future with fear, the enemy of creativity.

A downward cycle is set in motion. Concern about the future reduces creativity, reducing new business, which increases fear, further suppressing creativity. The more this cycle progresses, the more the Bureaucrat feels justified in cost cutting, reorganizing, and tightening controls.

In this fifth stage the organization has become more important than the individual. The individual now serves the organization, as anyone who has lived within a bureaucracy knows. There are five processes in motion that characterize organizational life in this stage: the centralization of power, the return to command decision making, machinelike behavior, the excess of specialization, and the creation of counterstructures.

The Centralization of Power Central staffs now define the methods and procedures for everything from how phones are answered to how supervisors spend their time.

An examination of those U.S. corporations that have successfully expanded through internal creativity—Johnson & Johnson, 3M, Procter & Gamble—reveals they have decentralized, and it is this process that has spurred innovation. For example, within 3M, managers can create new products and applications. They become champions and heroes of the business through creative development. While 3M does have a strong central research and development organization, more new products have come from field managers listening to their customers and developing innovative responses to their customers' needs.

Decentralization allows one to manage one's own business. This is one of the primary mechanisms for preserving the qualities of the Prophet and Barbarian, vision and decisive action.

But at this stage the executive will find high resistance to true decentralization. His staff and key executives, who wish to maintain control and who fundamentally do not trust their subordinate managers, will attempt to undermine it.

The Return to Command Decision Making During the Barbarian days, the dominant decision-making style was command. From the Building and Exploring Age to the Administrative Age, the dominant style was consultative and occasionally consensus. During the declining years of Bureaucracy and Aristocracy, the leaders are increasingly issuing orders to obtain compliance and action. The consultative style is not successful because subordinates don't understand their purpose. Consensus is impossible in the absence of common vision. The fear induced by the controlling systems destroys self-initiative, and now individuals must increasingly be ordered and instructed rather than relied upon.

Machinelike Behavior Administration creates orderliness and therefore efficiency. An excess of administration provides machinelike, mindless behavior and inefficiency.

The character of robotlike response, initially expected of employees in simple manufacturing jobs, also becomes a characteristic of managers. As controls and command authority increase fear, employees increasingly "do as they are told," avoid risk, and do not ask, "Why?" This behavior is unlikely to produce future business for the corporation. Managers act on orders, believing they can neither challenge nor change them. This deprives the corporation of the collective wisdom of its members. In this way the Bureaucratic organizations lose "self-determination."

During recent years I have observed a distressing trend among senior executives to mandate 5 percent to 10 percent cuts in expenses across the board. Their command to reduce expenses is passed downward with no consideration to which divisions are expanding, which are contracting, and which have other needs. The managers carrying out these decisions appear intent on engaging in no thoughtful dialogue that will force them to weigh one priority or concern over another. They would rather deny responsibility by saying, "The CEO said 10 percent across the board, and that's it."

The U.S. Congress engaged in this behavior with the passage of the Gramm-Rudman bill, which programs automatic reductions in spending.

Congress has concluded that it is unable to make wise decisions in consideration of facts, and in frustration it is willing to submit to mindless adherence to rules. Like the manager, the congressman can say to his constituents, "It doesn't matter what we think, the budget had to be cut by . . ."

The Excess of Specialization Specialization led to competence and efficiency, but with specialization motivation changes. Rather than deriving goals from common social purpose, goals are now increasingly based on moving up the ladder of one's own narrow field. The more "expert" one can become in a specialization, the more indispensable he is and the less others can challenge his "expert" decisions. Responsibility is now not for the whole, but for the narrow part, and the parts are less and less connected and increasingly esoteric.

This esotericism may be seen as a failure of creative individuals to complete the "withdrawal-return" process. They have withdrawn from the larger social context to enhance their knowledge, but they have failed to return to the larger social unit.

The Greeks had a word to describe the social offense of withdrawal from society in pursuit of esoteric knowledge. The word is that from which we derive the word *idiot*. The "idiot" was a superior personality who withdrew and lived for himself instead of putting his gifts to the service of the common good.

This is the offense commonly committed by corporate staff groups who pride themselves in "state of the art" knowledge and tools without thinking about how that knowledge can benefit the corporation.

I recently attended a meeting of twenty-six managers at a consumer products company. This major corporation has invested millions of dollars in the most up-to-date mainframe computers and the latest in manufacturing software. They also have a large staff of information systems specialists. The highlight of the meeting was a presentation by a plant manager about his experience starting up a new plant during which he relied entirely on mini- and microcomputer vendors and did not call upon the corporate information systems staff at all. When he had asked them for help, they told him it would take them three years to write the software and get the systems in place. So he circumvented the entire system and bought his own computer software. This experience was consistent with those of the other plant managers who had dealt with the corporate staff. They all wanted to know from the executives if they could do the same.

This was a failure of specialization resulting from a failure to understand who one's customer is. Everyone has a customer, internal or external. In this case the plant managers are customers of the corporate MIS department. However, the corporate staff did not feel any accountability to meet the requirements of their customers. It is the first requirement of effective corporate staff management to know its customer and his needs.

There are some emotional states in which creative thought is impossible, and the chief of these is the sense of helpless humiliation and anger which is produced in a sensitive nature by conscious inability to oppose or avoid the "insolence of office." Let any man who doubts it sit down for a day's work at the British Museum after being grossly insulted by someone whom he is not in a position to resist.
—GRAHAM WALLAS, 1858–1932

Creation of Counterstructures The psychological need for affiliation and empowerment will be fulfilled, if not through the primary organization, then through the creation of counterstructures. Unions are the fulfillment of the same psychological need that drives many entrepreneurs to start their own companies. Employees want to feel in control. Unions are created to fulfill this need when the corporation's leaders make their employees feel powerless.

Unions may appear during the Administrative Age, but it is during this fifth stage that they will increasingly demonstrate their power in opposition to Bureaucratic management. This will be the period of worst conflict, a response to a management who sees employees as one more cost factor in the financial equation. It is the failure to recognize employees as partners, friends, and trusted allies that creates the rebellious underclass within the society of the corporation.

You May Be in a Bureaucratic Age If . . .

. . . your company is growing more by acquisition than by new product creation.

. . . your company has reorganized more than once in the past three years.

. . . employees and managers alike feel that they can do little to alter the company's fortunes.

. . . managers and employees tend to talk about the "good old days" when things were exciting and fun.

. . . managing or fixing the systems and structure receives more time and attention than selling and producing.

CHALLENGES AND TASKS

The primary task of the organization in this stage is to renew the culture, to break the bonds of bureaucracy and free individual creativity suppressed by the weight of controls.

Renewal Through New Leadership The breakup of conglomerates by corporate raiders and the leveraged buy-out (LBO) by managers serve to cut bureaucracy and return the attention of managers to the real business of the business.

Sybron Corporation had navigated its way through most of the life cycle stages. Originally named the Ritter Pfaudler Corporation, Sybron made chemicals and processing and dental equipment. Revenues peaked in 1980. Chief Executive Herbert W. Jarvis had built up his corporate staff and life-style, detaching himself from the concerns of any particular division or the company's overall direction. With the stock price falling, he embarked on the typical Bureaucratic response, restructuring the business without thought to products or customers.

Saddled with the overhead of a bloated corporate staff and acquisition failures, division managers became increasingly frustrated and alienated.

Brian Bremer, a division president, says Sybron's leaders were "more concerned about taking vacations and getting new cars and refurbishing their offices than addressing the tough decisions."

Jarvis and four other corporate managers tried to take Sybron private in an LBO, but their own subordinate managers—feeling they would not benefit—outbid them after aligning with takeover specialists Forstmann Little. One of the division heads, Frank H. Jellinek, Jr., of Erie Scientific Co., initiated what would ultimately turn out to be the successful bid.

Jellinek and his family had sold Erie to Sybron in 1969 for stock that then traded around 40 and had subsequently fallen to 12. Sybron, he says, was "a giant joke. There had been gross management errors." Jellinek had stayed close to the products, services, and customers he knew. He even convinced one of his suppliers, Corning Glass Works, to participate in the buy-out.

After Forstmann Little took over Sybron, they brought in Kenneth F. Yontz, an executive vice president of the Allen-Bradley Company, as president. Yontz quickly sold off eleven Sybron divisions, providing the cash to pay off almost all of Sybron's debt. (Corporate value is almost always enhanced by the divestiture of nonintegrated divisions, with whom synergy cannot be expected and which cause executives to lose focus on their customers.) Only six divisions remained, and Yontz now turned his attention to increasing their value.

He did that by eliminating the corporate bureaucracy, cutting staff from 145 to 7. The corporate computer and information systems staff were eliminated. The remaining corporate personnel made do with a personal computer. Most of the accounting and administration were pushed down into the divisions, where the division managers were held accountable for their own costs rather than being saddled with huge corporate overhead.

Instead of spending his time in corporate meetings developing esoteric strategies, Yontz spent his time in the divisions, helping their managers develop their own improvement strategies. In the old days, a division manager had to get four or five signatures for a capital expenditure. Under the new system a division president received approval for a $600,000 new equipment expenditure in twenty-four hours. Now division managers felt they were genuine partners with their president and the new owners.

The results? In 1986 operating profit jumped to $54.7 million on sales of $499.3 million, up from $27.3 million on sales of $529.7 million in 1985.

Renewing Creativity Within Peter Drucker tells us the corporation exists for two purposes: innovation (of product) and marketing. When it fails at the first, it will be unable to succeed at the second. It is the nature of bureaucracy to stifle creativity. It is up to the leaders of the organization to free that creativity by pointing out the gap between where we are today and where we could be tomorrow. The members of the organization must have a clear vision of the future. A burning desire to accomplish a goal is the only way to break bureaucratic constraints. What is worth getting excited about, losing sleep over, sacrificing for? Why will you be proud to have served this company? You, the leader, must be able to answer these questions.

New Challenge—New Response The failure of creativity is also a failure to nurture and appreciate people of diverse inclinations. Prophets and Barbarians are each unique and nonconforming. They have little chance for survival in this Bureaucratic Age. They are creators, the antithesis of Bureaucrats.

Creativity is the recognition that new challenges require new responses. People who have not rigidly conformed to the old are more likely to recognize the new. Jesus was literally commenting on business when he said:

> *No man putteth a piece of new cloth into an old garment, for that which is put in to fill it up taketh from the garment, and the rest is made worse. Neither do men put new wine into old bottles—else the bottles break and the wine runneth out and the bottles perish; but they put new wine into new bottles, and both are preserved.*
>
> —MATTHEW IX, 16–17

Each successive challenge is the new wine, requiring a new solution.

Honda shows us one way this can be done. One of the core principles of its management philosophy is "to proceed always with youthfulness." Why youthfulness? It is a characteristic of the young to try things that are different from, perhaps even contrary to, the old way. If you are "proceeding always with youthfulness," you are constantly exploring new ways and frequently finding better ways.

Avoid a Condition of Ease Ease is the enemy of creativity. The Bureaucratic organization appears to be secure. It has huge assets, buildings, staffs, pension plans, and benefits. But we have seen that neither civilizations nor corporations are born out of a condition of ease. They are born out of a condition of challenge, and the more severe the challenge, the greater the impulse to creativity.

The leader who is able to regenerate bureaucracy must create the psychology of crisis. He or she must instill the urgency that speeds the pulse. It is the job of the regenerative leader to bring the crisis to the door of every individual and provide an avenue of response. Creativity, whether in new product development or on the factory floor, is enhanced by the thrill of striving for something of significance, something offering the reward of pride and self-esteem.

Breaking the Rigidity of Institutions Bureaucratic organizations need to redefine accountability to ensure that the largest-possible number of people feel responsible for the organization's fate. The imposition of centralized staff control has inhibited this accountability and caused decisions to rise to ever higher levels. I recently consulted with an organization of engineers who were responsible for the design and construction of multimillion-dollar structures. The engineers all had graduate degrees from prestigious universities. They were not, however, allowed to sign their name to *any* documents. All letters leaving the organization had to be signed by a manager two or three levels up. For the bureaucratic malaise to be broken, decision making and authority must be pushed down to those who are on the spot, in touch with the product.

To renew the corporate culture, it will have to go on a deliberate program of physical fitness. The *structures, systems, skills, style,* and *symbols* must be redefined. The leader must act as both the Prophet and Barbarian, restoring the vision and values yet taking decisive action to re-create the form.

The leader must establish a process of redesign in which the line managers, those who must implement and live with the outcome, are the people doing the redesign. And the process should be ongoing. The challenges an organization faces constantly change; its response to those challenges should, too.

This continual redesign process will keep the managers focused on basic principles such as defining customers and meeting customer requirements; minimizing layers and pushing decision making down to the lowest-possible level. It will prevent complacency and arrogance. It will instill the belief that it is management's job to be continually managing change, to be striving for higher levels of performance.

Renewing Social Unity The ultimate act that signals the breakdown of civilizations is an outbreak of internal discord, a civil war between factions and fiefdoms. The social disintegration of the society and of the corporation may be seen along both vertical and horizontal planes. The horizontal disintegration occurs in civilizations divided into increasing numbers of parochial states, engaging in internal competition that exhausts the energies of the society, increasing its vulnerability to external attack. As Toynbee tells us:

> Indeed, in no less than fourteen out of the sixteen cases in which we can pronounce with assurance that a broken-down civilization has brought the breakdown upon itself, we have found that a reckless indulgence in the crime of interstate warfare has been the main line of suicidal activity. [15]

The energies of the managers within ITT, U.S. Steel, and Bethlehem Steel during their declining years were exerted more against internal combatants than against outside competition.

The vertical disintegration of society is seen in the development of increasing classes. This layering results in an increasing psychological separation of leaders and followers. Roman society was clearly broken down into citizens and plebeians and many additional classes of conquered peoples who were controlled by Rome but had no chance at upward social mobility. In decaying corporations it is very common for the leadership class to be drawn from certain schools or professions, with the more common citizens aware that the door to the top is open only to the proper class.

The breakdown is accompanied by a schism between the leaders and the led. In a corporation the response is not a violent mutiny. Rather, capable employees simply leave and go where their talents will be put to better use.

Along with this increasing schism goes a degeneration of trust. With the breakdown in communication between classes, it is more and more difficult to create trust, and trust is the foundation upon which the relationship between leaders and led is built.

I have watched executives in several large industrial corporations struggle to regain that trust by making sincere pronouncements, visiting production facilities, and attempting to share their concerns. Sometimes these efforts are effective. However, the schism is real. It is not merely a matter of communication. The Bureaucratic leader does, in fact, live in a different world and holds to different perceptions. The well-orchestrated communication effort is soon undermined by decisions that demonstrate the Bureaucratic view varies greatly from the one on the production line. Change, not just communication, is required.

Chairman Mao sent all of the government office workers to toil in the fields for one year. Imagine if all the federal government employees were sent out from Washington to work in the fields, schools, factories, and hospitals. H. Ross Perot has suggested that the executive offices of General Motors should be closed and all executives moved out into the manufacturing plants, where they would have to mix with real people making real cars. The point of both Mao's and Perot's ideas is to eliminate the class alienation that causes revolution.

Managers must develop a sensitivity to the development of alienation or class distinctions and set up exercises by which those distinctions can be minimized. Don't wait for the revolution.

◆

The Aristocrat

Alienation and Revolution

I hold that a little rebellion, now and then, is a good thing, and as necessary in the political world as storms in the physical.

—THOMAS JEFFERSON

Management derives its power from its legitimacy, and in the Aristocratic Age legitimacy is lost. It is lost because the managers have stopped doing their job, that of leading, creating vision, social purpose, and unity. Peter Drucker has said:

Power has to be legitimate. Otherwise it has only force and no authority, is only might and never right. To be legitimate, power has to be grounded outside of itself in something transcending that is accepted as a genuine value. . . . If power is an end in itself, it becomes despotism, both illegitimate and tyrannical.[1]

139

And this is what happens in the Aristocratic Age.

During the recent past there have been numerous examples of Aristocracy in corporate America. The shareholder rebellion at Beatrice Foods and Continental Group shows what happens when Aristocratic management loses touch with its stockholders.

In fact, anywhere there is rebellion, look for the Artistocrat. Look at American auto companies, and you will find Aristocratic management following their own delusions rather than the desires of their fleeing customers. Look at United States Steel or Bethlehem Steel, and you will find Aristocrats so far removed from their employees that they could not hear their cries for dignity and leadership. Look at Beech-Nut Foods, and you will find Aristocrats more concerned with minor fluctuations on the profit-and-loss statement than the very lives of their infant customers. These are all cases of lost legitimacy and well-earned rebellion.

Legitimacy is a matter of perceptions, and it is the perceptions of the constituent groups that matter. In every relationship there must be a balance of power, a mutual concern and respect. When these mechanisms break down, leadership acts on its own interests, and contrary to the interests of its followers, rebellion inevitably results.

The disintegration of culture may appear as either an internal revolution or an attack by competing Barbarians. In either case, the cause is the same: the loss of social unity brought about by alienated leadership and the loss of legitimacy.

Aristocracy will not persist for long in a highly competitive environment, so it is not common in American corporations that face competitive forces. Competition requires creativity, responsiveness to customers, and competition for human resources. Aristocratic managers and companies can't survive in competitive environments.

Banks are perhaps the clearest example. For many years they were Aristocratic. They could be. Theirs was a highly regulated industry. But once the financial markets were deregulated, the noncreative nature of their leaders became obvious.

THE CHARACTER OF THE ARISTOCRAT

Webster's dictionary defines "aristocracy" as "government by a privileged minority, usually of inherited wealth. A privileged ruling class; upper class."

The Aristocrat appears highly civilized and has a rigid social protocol. But he does not produce or create goods or services; no new wealth is created as a result of his efforts. He has inherited the wealth produced by previous generations of productive managers and workers. He has inherited the corporation with large assets, products, people, and established markets. He will spend his time rearranging, trading, and manipulating the assets, but he is unlikely to create new ones. That is only done by creative leaders.

Robert Foman led E. F. Hutton through much of its rise and all of its fall. It is within the capacity of one individual to serve as the Barbarian and Builder yet become an Aristocrat when he achieves a condition of ease. In Foman's behavior, and the fall of E. F. Hutton, can be seen most of the basic flaws, in character and culture, that make up Aristocracy.

When Foman, then head of corporate finance on the West Coast, became chief executive in 1970, E. F. Hutton had revenues of $85 million and employed 1,275 account executives. Two years later he took the firm public, and between 1972 and 1982 its market share nearly tripled, 2,225 account executives were added, and revenues soared to $1.1 billion. From the seed of this rapid success emerged the conceit that would produce an equally dramatic decline.

The most public evidence of the fall came in 1985 when the firm pleaded guilty to two thousand counts of mail and wire fraud involving a $4 million check-kiting scheme. Foman pleaded the firm guilty to avoid indictment of certain top officers. This eventually led to the takeover of Hutton by Shearson-American Express and, for all practical purposes, the end of the firm. The real story, the cause rather than the effect, is to be found in the behavior and personality of the leader.

There was little in the way of a management at Hutton. As *Fortune* magazine reported:

Like a feudal lord, he banished organization, budgets, and planning from his domain. He hired and promoted whomever he wanted, including close friends. He personally reviewed the salaries and bonuses of more than 1,000 employees.[2]

One employee said:

His whole life was holding court, making all the large and small decisions. When Friday night at six o'clock rolled around, a tear would come down his cheek because he was wondering what the hell he was going to do till Monday. Outside of work, he was the loneliest man who ever lived.[3]

Hutton never entered the Administrative period. It went directly from the third stage of Building and Exploring to Aristocracy. Although Foman was an Administrator by training, he never created the administrative controls and management processes that other brokerage firms, such as Merrill Lynch, began to develop during this period. Hutton's senior officers were more skilled at deal making than constructing systems. Hutton did not know which brokers were making or losing money. While Hutton paid higher commissions than other brokerage firms, it had no expense control. One investment banker ran up $900,000 in travel and entertainment expenses in 1986.

The inability to separate the person from the position, the personality from the power, is a symptom of Aristocracy. Robert Foman's ego and needs were confused with the decisions of the business. He admits that he was fond of "pretty young girls" and reportedly put girlfriends on the payroll and bedded a number of Hutton employees. A top officer said that Foman "considered it the spoils of war." When asked about his appearance in *M* magazine with his arms around two girls young enough to be his granddaughters, he responded, "They're decorative, nice to look at, they have keen senses of humor. I don't understand why people got upset. I can't help it if I appear in the papers with young girls." And, symbolic of his material obsession, he invested $100 million in a new office tower when the company was losing money. Inside, it became known as "Foman's last erection."

In 1986 the firm lost $90 million but spent an incredible $30 million to send its best-producing brokers and their wives on all-expenses-paid trips. Two corporate jets stood ready to fly Foman to a Hutton apartment in Paris, London, or San Francisco. And when the fall finally came, Hutton's board voted itself $2.5 million in retirement benefits. Peter Ueberroth, board member and baseball commissioner, alone pocketed $1 million, including $500,000 for leading the negotiations to sell the firm he had failed to "direct" as a member of its board of *directors*. Most employees were forgotten in the final division of the spoils. Most were not allowed to sell Hutton shares held in trust for them and got nothing more than unemployment checks.

The closing chapter in the saga was in keeping with the company culture. One executive said, "People around here believed that if they could get away with something, they should do it." That belief could also be found among the nobility and court of the French kings before the Revolution. Unlike the French Revolution, however, the Aristocrats of E. F. Hutton did not meet the guillotine. Instead they met the further self-indulgence of the golden parachutes.

It is the character of the Aristocrat to sincerely believe that his position has earned him the right to total self-indulgence. And at the same time, there is a total denial of responsibility and failure of empathy for those below. Foman believed he was due all of the luxury and personal pleasures his office could buy. Yet while the stockholders were losing $90 million in one year and a wealth-producing institution was being destroyed, the leader could say, "Did I let the firm down? Did I let the employees down? No, I don't think so." This is the denial of reality, the corruption of values, the arrogance and loss of empathy that is Aristocracy!

And it is the total system, the failure of checks and balances, the failure of reward and punishment for serving or destroying the social good, that breeds and permits the escape of the Aristocratic criminal who has robbed the stockholder, employee, customers, and public at large. All social revolutions, the American, French, and Russian revolutions, were the result of such failed systems.

"Has God forgotten all I have done for him?"
—Louis XIV

Aristocracy is an emotional state. The creative leader who is contributing new wealth through his efforts feels a kinship with those who work beside or beneath him. The Aristocrat, though, has too long been removed from those below and has lost any sympathy for his followers. Woodrow Wilson understood:

> I do not believe that any man can lead who does not act, whether it be consciously or unconsciously, under the impulse of a profound sympathy with those whom he leads—a sympathy which is insight—an insight which is of the heart rather than of the intellect.

The leader's focus, his motivation, has now shifted from serving others to serving self. In the later days of a society the leaders become obsessed with material self-gratification. This obsession is largely due to the loss of gratification normally derived from productive work. There is satisfaction to be derived from sawing and sanding wood into a piece of furniture, from designing, testing, and watching a mechanical object come to life, from listening to a customer and sincerely striving to meet his needs. All of these pleasures are lost to the Aristocrat. Now, the rewards come from the appearance of wealth. The irony is that the Aristocrat is not achieving greater satisfaction than a productive individual. The supervisor whose team sets a production record is undoubtedly achieving a higher level of satisfaction than the Aristocrat purchasing the Gulfstream IV or the new limousine or conducting meetings at the country club. The Aristocrat has simply lost touch, forgotten the meaningful satisfactions that come from a job well done.

I recently traveled to Boston for a speaking engagement held at the Marquis de Lafayette Hotel, an inn decorated in grand style: great chandeliers, polished brass, deep carpets, and fine paintings —all the symbols of wealth and quality. Unfortunately, the service was an abomination. I arrived at 9:30 P.M. with a confirmed reservation to find other people, also with confirmed reservations, waiting ahead of me for their rooms. After waiting at the reception desk for ten minutes, I was told that there would be at least an hour wait because the maids were still cleaning the rooms. Unfortunately, as I later discovered, this was not an isolated incident.

The next day I was pleased to be in a simple and modest Holiday Inn at the Hartford Airport, where the young staff greeted their guests with friendly enthusiasm, offered each a red apple, and provided prompt and efficient service.

Our dangerous class is not at the bottom, it is near the top of society. Riches without law are more dangerous than is poverty without law.
— HENRY WARD BEECHER, 1873

The crime now is that the Aristocrats are diverting the corporate resources required to maintain a competitive position. The diversion of funds from research and development and capital improvement to hallucinatory acquisitions and the construction of elaborate office buildings are the Aristocrat's crimes. The absconding of funds from the productive employees or stockholders of Beatrice, Bendix, or Revlon is no more defensible than the behavior of autocratic rulers, such as President Marcos of the Philippines, who have stashed in Swiss bank accounts money taxed from their pitiful and underfed populations. It is a symptom of leaders out of touch with their reason for existence, unchecked by effective balance of power.

Surely there is no more outrageous example of Aristocrats at work than the executives of Beatrice. The chairman, in his job for a mere seven months, negotiated for his company to be taken over. One of the provisions of the deal was that he would receive a "golden parachute" worth several million dollars. Similarly generous deals were provided for his court of surrounding executives. This executive did not create, produce, improve, sell, or manage one single product. All of those products were created, produced, and sold by others. But they experienced none of the gain from the chairman's exchange of assets from one pair of hands to another. This act served to further disillusion operating managers who felt that they were abandoned and used by those from whom they expected leadership.

The wealth of a society is defined by the number and quality of goods and services available for consumption per capita. It is the function of business to create those goods and services, and it is to these ends that assets are legitimately employed. A dollar may be invested in new product research or a lottery ticket. It is true that people may be employed in the management of the lottery, and it is true that someone will attain great wealth as a result. But the net assets of the society are not in any way increased. They are, in fact, diminished by the redirection of capital and human energy from those activities that produce new products and services. The failure of the Aristocrat is, in part, a failure to employ capital in a way that enhances the wealth of society. During the creative stages of corporate development, leaders used capital to create product and marketing innovations, the real purpose of business. Now capital is employed in ventures outside of the primary business purpose. The Aristocrat's belief that he has a right to use other people's money in any way he sees fit is one of the many forms of arrogance afflicting the culture.

The theme is an old one: do you accept that a higher class has been granted the right to make decisions without accountability, or do you trust the "common people" to do what's right? Thomas Jefferson observed the two courses in society:

> Men by their constitutions are naturally divided into two parties: (1) Those who fear and distrust the people, and wish to draw all powers from them into the hands of the higher classes. (2) Those who identify themselves with the people, have confidence in them, cherish and consider them as the most honest and safe.

In every country these two parties exist; and in every one where they are free to think, speak, and write, they will declare themselves.

In the Aristocratic country or company, the first course has won out over the second.

You May Be an Aristocrat If . . .

. . . you manage an organization that has not successfully developed and marketed new products or services for many years, and your only expectation for growth is through acquisition.

. . . most of your time is spent on financial matters, strategic planning, and restructuring the organization, not with those who produce or sell the product or service.

. . . your offices are plush with expensive artwork, you have limousine service, and you spend a lot of time at expensive social gatherings, for business, of course.

. . . you feel that only you and a small circle of advisers are capable of understanding the strategy of the corporation.

THE ARISTOCRAT IN HISTORY

The defeat of the Aztecs and their leader, Montezuma II, by a much inferior force has been the cause of wonder for hundreds of years. It well illustrates how leaders defeat themselves in the declining stage of the life cycle curve.

The Aztec culture was superior in many ways to their European conquerors. The Aztecs were highly advanced in the arts, sciences, and agriculture. They possessed elaborate architecture and an extended hierarchy of social classes and dominated conquered provinces. They also possessed a large, proven military, against which Hernan Cortes marched with six hundred soldiers.

During the declining years of every civilization, the spirit of religion is perverted. The grandeur of the idols, temples, and television studios become more significant than the spiritual substance they are meant to serve. The Aztecs built immense and beautiful temples, but their form of worship required the most brutal forms of human sacrifice with hundreds of victims put to death daily. By the Aztecs' own account, the founding god, Quetzalcoatl, the "Feathered Snake," had fallen from glory. The sun god, Tezcatlipoc, and the rain god, Tlaloc, who demanded the blood of human sacrifice, were in control.

The Aztecs believed themselves to be the "people of the Sun." Their duty was to wage war in order to provide the sun with its nourishment. The survival of the universe depended upon the offerings of blood and hearts to the sun, a notion the Aztecs extended to all deities in their pantheon. Human sacrifice became the most important feature of their ritual. Death by sacrifice was considered a guaranteed way of gaining a happy eternal life. It was therefore stoically accepted or even voluntarily sought. It was into this environment that Cortes marched.

There can be no mistaking the personality of Hernan Cortes. When he landed on the coast of Mexico on February 18, 1519, he had 11 ships, 508 soldiers, about 100 sailors, and perhaps most important—16 horses. Cortes succeeded because he was willing to do what no previous Spanish explorer had done. He demanded discipline within his forces. With one dramatic stroke he did more to create that discipline than any rules or orders could achieve. He set his ships afire, eliminating any possibility of retreat. Not the act of an Administrator!

Montezuma first tried to appease the invader by sending gifts and a letter urging Cortes to turn back. But the material power of the Aztecs was about to meet the spiritual vitality of the Spaniards. Cortes marched on, carrying the cross and with priests ready for converts. Here we have the clear confrontation of one people, who by their own account had lost their god, by another prepared to die for theirs.

Montezuma consulted with his council but was unable to elicit a consensus on a course of action. He hesitated to move without their approval. The Spaniards, who were outnumbered by at least a hundred to one, marched into the city unopposed. They demanded gold and jewels, showed complete disdain for the Aztecs' religion, and still Montezuma remained passive. Finally his brother led a revolt, and in the battle the Spaniards called upon Montezuma to declare a truce, at which point he was stoned to death by his own people.

Cortes's victory, like those of the Huns and Visigoths against the Romans or the Muslims' later conquest of Spain, was not so much the story of a great military triumph as the story of alienation and disintegration of the conquered society. It was the story of an Aristocratic culture, in which the leaders were alienated from their own people and lacked the ability to take decisive action. It is not difficult to argue that the conquest by the aggressive Barbarian auto, steel, and electronic producers from the Orient against the likes of General Motors, General Electric, and U.S. Steel represents not so much a brilliant victory, but the inevitable result of Aristocratic management suffering from the same illness.

If the fall of Montezuma was an example of decay leading to conquest by external barbarians, the Protestant Reformation, the rebellion against the Church of Rome, was an example of decay leading to internal rebellion.

In *The March of Folly*, Barbara W. Tuchman defines folly as the pursuit of policy contrary to self-interest. This seems also to define the behavior of Aristocrats. She includes in her catalog of famous follies the behavior from the period 1470 to 1530 of the Renaissance popes, who, by their complete separation from the true purpose of their Prophet and their alienation from their followers, provided the stimulus for the Protestant Reformation. In their conduct can be seen the derangement of mind that overcomes those who achieve a status beyond accountability for the consequences of their behavior.

Pope Sixtus IV, who ascended to the papacy in 1471, is a vivid example. Soon after becoming pope, he shocked the public by appointing two of his nephews, both in their twenties, as cardinals. But this was only the beginning. Before he was through, he had appointed three more nephews and a grandnephew cardinals, made another a bishop, and gave archiepiscopal sees to children only eight and eleven, both sons of princes.

Sixtus only began a trend that was reinforced by his successor, Innocent VIII, who was innocent of very little that was unholy. He was the son of a wealthy Genoese family and was elected to the

College of Cardinals after fathering several illegitimate children. He became pope only because of a deadlock between two more ambitious candidates. Innocent was best known for his devotion to his son Franceschetto, whose marriage to the daughter of Lorenzo de Medici, the great Florentine merchant, he arranged. The pope celebrated his son's wedding with a party in the Vatican so elaborate that he was forced to mortgage the papal tiara and other treasures to pay for it. Innocent's most important appointment to the College of Cardinals was Franceschetto's new brother-in-law, Giovanni de Medici, fourteen. Not surprisingly, Giovanni would go on to become Pope Leo X.

The College of Cardinals was appointed by the popes, and they in turn elected the popes. It was a closed system that served to reinforce its own values, values that had drifted increasingly away from the teachings of Christ. Any closed system, in which the members are appointed by the leaders and then the appointed elect more leaders (much like the chairman appointed by the board), is likely to become corrupt because it is not *required* to respond to external forces.

Alexander VI followed Innocent and did little but carry the depravity to new heights. Alexander was Cardinal Rodrigo Borgia, elected at sixty-two after thirty-five years as cardinal. He is said to have purchased the papacy outright from two chief rivals who received four muleloads of bullion.

> His character, habits, principles or lack of them, uses of power, methods of enrichment, mistresses and seven children were well enough known to his colleagues in the College to evoke from young Giovanni de Medici at his first conclave, the comment on Borgia's elevation to the Papacy, "Flee, we are in the hands of a wolf."[4]

Alexander staged bullfights in the Piazza of St. Peter. He went slightly beyond the accepted norms of behavior when he took as mistress Vanozza de Cataneis, nineteen, who succeeded her mother in that role. He married her to a member of a wealthy family, as he had married off her mother. Borgia himself, as recorded by apparently objective observers, boasted of these relationships.

> Burchard, the Master of Ceremonies, was neither antagonist nor apologist. The impression from his toneless diary of Alexander's Papacy is of continuous violence, murders in churches, bodies in the Tiber, fighting of factions, burning and looting, arrests, tortures and executions, combined with scandal, frivolities and continuous ceremony, reception of ambassadors, princes and sovereigns, obsessive attention to garments and jewels, protocol of processions, entertainments and horse races with cardinals winning prizes—with a running record throughout of the costs and finances of the whole. . . . Religion, except for an occasional reference to Alexander's observances of Lenten fasts or his concern to maintain the purity of Catholic doctrine by censorship of books, is barely mentioned.[5]

This pattern of behavior persisted during the reign of the next six popes. They not only lacked celibacy, they lacked discretion. Their vice was common knowledge. There were several decades during which the call for reform was a constant topic of discussion among lower-level priests and secular rulers. Not only were the popes called upon to reform, but Charles V of France led an army to demand it.

Rebellion against alienated leadership occurs in many forms. Some simply lose their faith. Others fight against the present leaders to reform the institution. Others may form alternative, competing institutions. The Aristocracy of the Vatican produced all three forms of rebellion. The Protestant Reformation, of course, was the great split, the disunity in the social fabric of the society, created entirely by the alienation of its leaders.

Would there ever have been a Reformation were it not for the behavior of the Renaissance popes? There is no way to know. But we do know that it was an internal rebellion aimed at the leaders of the Church. And if we examine every significant rebellion, including the American and French revolutions, we find the same pattern. In every case there were Aristocrat leaders, deaf to the cries of concern among their followers and separated by wealth and grandeur from those on whose loyalty they depended.

THE BUSINESS ARISTOCRAT

While truly Aristocrat corporations are not common, there are numerous tendencies toward Aristocracy. This tendency is partly responsible for the recent rash of corporate takeovers. An examination of corporations subjected to hostile takeovers reveals that they are likely to have neither social purpose nor a strong vision of their future. Their assets are undervalued because they are not paying the stockholders the dividends the core business is generating. The managers are addicted to the habit of asset growth and have spent the earnings on acquisitions that they proceed to manage uncreatively, further diminishing the value of the stock.

> *What's going on in companies all over the country these days is absurd. It's like a corporate welfare state. We're supporting managements who produce nothing. No, it's really worse than that. Not only are we paying these drones not to produce, but we're paying them to muck up the works.*
> —CARL ICAHN, CORPORATE RAIDER AND CEO, TWA

The Continental Group, Inc., formerly Continental Can Company, lost sight of its core food and beverage container business and acquired insurance, energy, and natural resource businesses that the leaders neither understood nor were committed to. Management measured its success by the company's size, not its net value. The company had looked like a cash cow, but a consulting firm had confirmed what the leaders suspected: the can and packaging business, though it made a reasonable return on investment, was not an area of high growth. The consultants recommended the classic portfolio management prescription—that the returns be invested in new ventures that could achieve higher returns and growth. So Continental Group went out and bought a Florida gas company just when energy stocks were selling at their highest multiple. Then they purchased Life of Virginia. While the acquisitions increased the company's size, it also increased debt. And genuine shareholder value was not increased in the process.

What happened to the relationship between executives and the managers out in the manufacturing plants in Walla Walla, Washington, and fifty other plants around the company? Said one plant manager:

> It is no secret that the leaders of this company are ashamed of the word "can." We used to be The Can Company! We were proud of it. We were the best damned can company in the world! I used to get up in the morning and come to work proud because we were the best in the business and we knew it down on the shop floor and they knew it at company headquarters. Today, you have to search through the company's annual report to find any mention of the can business. The executives never come down to the plant. They spend their time in their fancy new office building in Stanford talking to investment bankers and consultants. We've lost our pride. You can feel it.

The managers in Continental Group's core business were genuinely angry at their leadership. There were the anonymous letters to executives venting the feelings of abandonment. There was a loss of young and talented managers. But the leaders did not respond because they could rationalize to themselves that these lower-level managers could not understand the grand strategy, the need to redeploy assets. They could explain to themselves that "business is tough and you have to do things that people don't like. You can't be soft." And it is all this sort of self-talk that serves to isolate leaders from those they lead.

The Aristocrat of the modern corporation isolates himself psychologically and intellectually with false arguments about the nature of business and his job. He engages in the "Nixon White House syndrome." He believes that the mob shouting outside his windows, the mob that once were his followers, lack his high perspective, and he, therefore, does not need to respond to their complaints. He says the same things to himself that the Renaissance popes must have been muttering when they heard the pleas for reform. Once any person refuses to respond to feedback from those to whom he is responsible, his defeat is inevitable.

That's what happened at Continental Can. The unsuccessful acquisitions drove down the stock price, and the company became a takeover target. Following the takeover, senior executives were dismissed and the acquisitions sold. Now the Continental Can Company is once again "The Can Company." It no longer deploys its profits to enter sexy new businesses. It just continues to make money and serve its customers well.

Aristocrats, perhaps because they have inherited their assets, are not emotionally attached to them. They are not "can men" or "steel men" or "oil men." They claim to be professional managers, but they lay a false claim. Barbarians are professional managers, crude and rough as they may be. They are professional when they are exhibiting the leadership style that moves their organization forward. Builders and Explorers, developing the specialized competence of production and selling, are professional managers. And true Administrators creating the mechanism of order are also professional managers. But the Aristocrat is not a manager at all; he is a pretender to the throne.

Over the past twenty years we have been creating an Aristocratic culture within the major business schools. The top MBAs come into the corporation prepared, not to do productive work, but to take their place as Aristocrats in training at high salaries. A few years ago I was at the Wharton Business School to interview graduating MBAs. I was having an informal discussion with a group of six or seven of them, and I asked them to tell me what their idea of a perfect job would be. Every one picked a job in either financial management and/or strategic planning. I asked if anyone wanted to work in production or sales and marketing. Not only were they not interested, they reacted as if I had insulted them by suggesting that they would lower themselves to actually engage in producing or selling. Our business schools have been producing students with strangely warped views. The heart of business is producing and selling, not financial management or strategic planning.

History does not repeat, but general trends do. Both within companies and civilizations, the disintegration of a society is preceded by a period in which wealth is achieved by the manipulation of paper related to assets, rather than by producing new assets. As writer Adam Smith recently pointed out:

> The Street money these days is made from pieces of paper—futures, options, tax shelters, moving corporate divisions from one balance sheet to another. That activity need not produce additional mousetraps. In the 1920s the games were played with utilities and holding companies. Pyramids were erected, companies owning companies owning companies, and the bootleg bubbly flowed until it all vanished. [6]

Before the fall of Rome, before the fall of the stock market in 1929, and before the fall of U.S. Steel and other large corporations, the senior executives were preoccupied not with the quality of production, creative selling, or development of new products, but with the cleverness of financial manipulations.

HOW TO GET ALONG WITH AN ARISTOCRAT

If You Work for an Aristocrat . . .

. . . if possible, quit. You are better off working for someone from whom you can learn to make productive contributions and who will reward your productive efforts. If the company is Aristocratic, you are living on borrowed time.

. . . if you can't quit, consider the Aristocrat's objectives and direction, but devise your own objectives and direction independently. He is not likely to give much credence to efforts to create or improve the actual business. You should pursue this on your own and hope that the Aristocrat's successor appreciates your efforts.

If an Aristocrat Works for You . . .

. . . you should be ashamed of yourself. Why is he there? Give him six months to change. If he doesn't, get rid of him!

. . . ask him very specific questions about his efforts to improve the business, the quality of products, services, and marketing, and ask him for his specific plans for creative developments.

THE ORGANIZATION OF THE ARISTOCRAT

In the Bureaucratic stage the company's organization was seen as its key to success. The Bureaucrat was constantly employing experts to design the latest structures and systems that would provide the solution to the declining growth. Now the managers have lost hope that any reorganization will renew vitality. During the Administrative and Bureaucratic stages, the corporation is a relatively secure environment. Now the only means available to the leaders to maintain a profit margin is cost reduction, and they go after this with a vengeance. Because they have no ideas for creating new products or services, they will push the only lever they know. This is a time when the heads of corporate staff are frequently rolling down the well-carpeted halls.

Fear has become a dominant force. Managers and employees are searching for safety and security. Entrepreneurial risk taking is almost impossible in an organization in which everyone is worrying about losing their job. Fear produces conformance and avoidance behavior, not initiative and risk taking. This negative psychology further propels the enterprise toward its doom.

Lower- and middle-level managers in the Aristocrat stage have given up on the idea of taking risks to gain competitive advantage. They are playing it safe. They are building their relationships with those at higher levels of power by mimicking their decisions and priorities as closely as they can. While this may help them survive, it guarantees uncreative decisions.

Given all this, whom does the Bureaucratic or Aristocratic organization attract? The daring young entrepreneurs? Of course not. It is those seeking the comfort of security and steady progress up the innumerable ladders of organization. These individuals who are attracted to the organization are not likely to serve as a force for change. They are likely to reinforce the culture and fit comfortably into the complacency and ritual. There is now a human dynamic of attraction and rejection that further guarantees the organization's fate. The mediocre are attracted, while the creative are rejected.

> Charles A. Beard (1874–1948), asked if he could summarize the lessons of history in a short book, said he could do it in four sentences:
> 1. Whom the gods would destroy, they first make mad with power.
> 2. The mills of God grind slowly, but they grind exceedingly small.
> 3. The bee fertilizes the flower it robs.
> 4. When it is dark enough, you can see the stars.

The primary cause of failure is the social disintegration within. Both horizontal and vertical schisms have become epidemic during the late years. The "classes" of executives, middle-level managers, lower-level managers, and workers, now all have a distinct identity. Each views the other with suspicion and fails to communicate. Disunity is quickly followed by internal warfare between the classes. Bethlehem Steel and U.S. Steel both came to their knees, in part because of the failure to invest in new technology, but also because of strikes that were not over money but were caused by the complete failure of communication and trust between employees and their management.

Arnold Toynbee described the disintegration of a civilization:

> This is only what we should expect; for we have found already that the ultimate criterion and the fundamental cause of the breakdown which precede disintegrations is an outbreak of internal discords through which societies forfeit their faculty for self-determination."[7]

You May Be Living in an Aristocratic Age If . . .

. . . there is a complete separation in perception, expectations, and communication between those workers and managers who produce and sell and those who claim to be the leaders of the corporation.

. . . a great deal of the time and energy is spent in internal warfare, both between horizontal units and vertical "classes."

. . . there is an almost constant process of reorganizing.

. . . there is continual effort to cut costs, hold down wages, and the "leaders" are constantly warning of the gravity of the situation, yet their own compensation is increasing with no apparent relationship to the fate of the business.

CHALLENGES AND TASKS

Rebellion is now the challenge and the task. Evolutionary, intelligent change has become exceedingly unlikely. Leadership has become mad with power and has neither eyes to see nor ears to hear.

The Declaration of Independence, among the finest documents ever written, puts forth a rational argument for the revolution against Aristocratic rule. The Founding Fathers experienced and saw clearly the inability of Aristocrats to alter their course. They knew there was no just path other than rebellion. Many who consider themselves the strongest defenders of the "American way" understand it least. They too often fear change, when it was the process of change that created this country.

> That to secure these rights, governments are instituted among men, deriving their power from the consent of the governed; that, whenever any form of government becomes destructive of these ends, it is the right of the people to alter or to abolish it, and to institute a new government, laying its foundation on such principles, and organizing its power in such form, as to them shall seem most likely to effect their safety and happiness. Pru-

dence, indeed, will dictate that governments long established, should not be changed for light and transient
causes. . . . But, when a long train of abuses and usurpations, pursuing invariably the same objective, evinces
a design to reduce them under absolute despotism, it is
their right, it is their duty, to throw off such government
and to provide new guards for their future security. . . .
The history of the present King of Great Britain is a
history of repeated injuries and usurpations, all having,
in direct object, the establishment of an absolute tyranny
over these States.

The Declaration of Independence lists the abuses and recalls
the "humble" efforts of the subjects to redress those grievances and
the failure of the king to respond. It is this pattern that inevitably
causes rebellion.

Are corporations and their constituents analogous to governments and their subjects? Ultimately, the right to conduct business
is contingent upon the will of the constituents, the customers, employees, and stockholders, just as the right to govern is contingent
upon the will of the governed. The principle that authority derives
its power from those at the bottom is fundamental to both free
enterprise and free government. Just as the people may rebel
against bad government, so too are the corporation's constituents
capable of their own revolt.

THE REBELLION OF THE EMPLOYEES

As civilizations crumble the masses become increasingly un-
ruly. The company was probably unionized during the Administrative or Bureaucratic Age, when the focus of senior managers drifted
away from productive work to the strategies and structures that
surround work. Workers perceive the change and become alienated.

When the leaders had a strong sense of purpose, they were
close to the work, and the workers were motivated. They were
motivated because they were respected and were doing something

regarded as important. Now they are viewed as a cost of doing business, something difficult to control.

The motivation and creativity of the employees is lost, and it will not be regained by minor manipulations of control or compensation systems. It will only be regained when *management* itself regains its creativity, its sense of purpose, and when it again develops genuine affection for productive work and productive workers.

> *There is something very unnatural and odious in a government a thousand leagues off. A whole government of our own choice, managed by persons whom we love, revere, and can confide in, has charms in it for which men will fight.*
> —JOHN ADAMS, 1776

Employees will rebel first with their feet. I recently consulted with a major corporation in which the leaders lost interest in the core business and initiated a restructuring. While some restructuring may have been necessary, it was done piecemeal, with announcements of changes in staffing, organization, and strategy made every few months over a period of three years. The employees and managers became so demoralized that they literally spent a third of their time sitting around talking about the meaning of each change and attempting to predict future changes. Several of the most capable and ambitious managers quit in frustration.

There is simply no way to calculate the financial value of talented people. We can certainly assume that the most capable managers are among the greatest value to the organization. And it is inevitably true that they will be the first to leave in frustration. Just as it is the best writers, dancers, and scientists who flee the Soviet Union for a culture that will support their creativity, so too will the best flee the Aristocratic corporation.

Rebellion can be seen in other ways. People will withdraw from their jobs. These found in the most meaningless jobs often become the most avid sports fans precisely because their energies require diversion. Those companies with the least-involved employees are those with leaders least involved in their employees' work.

Finally, employees rebel in the most obvious ways: direct opposition in the form of strikes. Of course there are economic issues that prompt strikes, and the process of collective bargaining is legitimate. However, the first cause of unions is the bureaucratization of management, which leads to the bureaucratization of the work force. The second cause of strikes is the growing schism between leaders and followers.

The meaning of "the Delta family feeling" is the preservation of unity between members of the organization regardless of rank. It implies that the interests of one are the interests of all. It implies a recognition of common purpose and fate. The employees at Delta have never rebelled. On their own initiative, they bought their company a Boeing 767, the *Spirit of Delta*, to demonstrate their appreciation. It is for this reason that Delta consistently achieves outstanding customer preference ratings and excellent financial performance.

THE REBELLION OF CUSTOMERS

Recently, the Cadillac division of General Motors has been doing little but losing market share to the likes of Mercedes-Benz, BMW, Jaguar, and even Honda's Acura in the industry's most profitable segment. One senior Cadillac executive's analysis of the problem was that Cadillacs looked too much like other GM cars. He announced that they would add fender and bumper extensions on their new cars to give them a more distinctive look. This, he felt, would improve their market share. But this executive does not understand the motivations of buyers of high-priced cars. The driver of a Mercedes-Benz, BMW, or Jaguar wants, and will pay for, superior engineering. It is not appearance. It's quality he is after. GM executives have simply lost touch with their customers and lost their legitimacy. It will take a decade, and perhaps even a generation, of solid performance before they can reclaim it.

Aristocrats typically seek to limit competition, sensing their own vulnerability. In a more healthy age the attack from external competition proved stimulating. Now its risks are unacceptable, and the Aristocrat is more likely to withdraw from the combat than risk the defeat of competition. The strategy of many large corporations to limit their businesses to those in which they possess a dominant market share virtually guarantees and assumes a non-risk-taking, non-entrepreneurial culture.

Many large companies have been trapped by their dominance. They arrogantly assumed their dominant market position provided them with a critical advantage. Rather, it proved their greatest disadvantage. Old food chains that thought they knew the right way to plan a supermarket were outpaced by fast-moving competitors; the Howard Johnson's that once was the dominant roadside restaurant has been overtaken by a horde of Barbarians with a completely different outlook on the business; IBM, although definitely not yet Aristocratic, may be on the edge of this same abyss.

The leaders of the Aristocratic organization have completely delegated the task of production, marketing, and sales. They have lost an understanding of the customer. They have such faith in their past accomplishments that when the customer's preferences and habits change they do not notice.

THE REBELLION OF THE STOCKHOLDERS

In large publicly traded companies, the ability of stockholders to rebel is the essential ingredient preserving the efficiency of the free market economy. Stockholders rebel first by divesting, driving down the stock price. The right to sell stock to a higher bidder is the only protection the legitimate owners have against those who have abused their position by misdirecting the stockholders' funds.

The mechanism of the board of directors has, in too many cases, become a sham, much like the election of a single slate of candidates in communist countries. The directors are nominated by management, serve at the pleasure of management, and then elect management. They are the College of Cardinals of the Renaissance popes. The system of directorship of public companies is on the verge of breaking down because it has largely become a closed system, and all closed systems suffer due to isolation from critical feedback. To the degree that the directors, and therefore management itself, are not serving at the pleasure of stockholders, they have lost their legitimacy. They are socialists in disguise. They do not believe in the free market, the individual investor's ability to make capital utilization decisions, or they would pay out the capital earned by their core business to their investors and allow them to make their own decisions.

Sir James Goldsmith, who has taken over several companies, views the alliance between the American corporate establishment, labor leaders, and government bureaucrats as analogous to the English class system and to the French bureaucracy, institutions he despises for their stifling effect on people's creativity. His intention, he claims, in attempting the ultimately unsuccessful acquisition of Goodyear was to cause it to refocus on its core business in tires and sell its disparate pieces to companies expert in those fields. He believed he could remake Goodyear into an entrepreneurial company with a focused and positive vision of its future.

The economy of the United States will benefit by the current restructuring of companies now, because the majority of the changes made are divestiture of nonintegrated businesses and the acquisition of businesses that can be integrated. Exxon's purchase of business units that could not be integrated with its energy business (office equipment, Reliance Electric) not only were bad investments, but diverted management attention from their primary responsibility. They have now sold those businesses. Goodyear is selling its aerospace and other nonintegrated businesses. There is a movement away from size for size sake. Business is becoming less concentrated and, therefore, more manageable. The share of assets held by the twenty-five largest nonfinancial companies dropped from seventeen percent in 1970 to 13 percent in 1984.

Most recent studies of mergers argue against their value to either stockholders or the economy. A study by Dennis C. Mueller of the University of Maryland and Ellen B. Magenheim of Swarthmore College followed seventy-eight acquisitions between 1976 and 1981 and found an average cumulative loss in market value of 16 percent over three years. F. Michael Scherer of Swarthmore studied industrial mergers and found that the merged company eventually lost about 40 percent of the market share the two companies had claimed separately. He also found that the typical merger experienced declining profitability for the eight years following its consummation.

What is clear from all studies is that mergers and acquisitions of nonintegrated businesses rarely add value. What does benefit both stockholders and the economy is the creation and maintenance of business units in which the managers are closely in touch with their core business, fighting for their survival and market share, behaving in a way that demonstrates commitment to all of their constituent groups. If they don't do this, they are inviting stockholder rebellion.

◆

The Synergist Prescription

From the clash of differing opinions comes the spark of truth.
—BAHA'U'LLAH, A PERSIAN PROPHET

Decline is not inevitable—only probable. Our challenge is to break the natural cycle of rise and fall by finding the mix of leadership qualities that will allow human energy to focus on both internal cooperation and external competition. If we do, the corporation will not decline, it will thrive.

A Synergist is a leader who has escaped his or her own conditioned tendencies toward one style and has incorporated the different styles of leadership that are needed as the corporation goes through its life cycle. The best-managed mature companies are Synergistic. They are a balance and blend of the characteristics of the Prophet, Barbarian, Builder, Explorer, and Administrator. But, most important, the Synergist is one who can create social unity.

165

The principle of yin and yang operates in all arenas of life. There is a time to emphasize one quality over the other and a time to seek a balance between the two opposing forces. The Synergist is the manager at the fulcrum, sometimes adding weight to one end, sometimes the other, always sensitive, always adjusting to hold the forces in balance. It is this balancing act that preserves the vitality and health of a mature company. It is preserved by the Synergist's ability to withstand the pressure of opposing forces, recognizing that if someone out on one end of the fulcrum is screaming that he is about to tip to his doom, the fulcrum simply may need slight adjustment. In this age the Synergist may also blend the qualities of East and West, released from the limited perspectives of one set of cultural biases.

Where can we find an example of such a blend—a large, successful, growing, creative company with strong social cohesion crossing national boundaries? We can find it in Marysville, Ohio.

Honda of America Manufacturing, Inc., should in no way be confused with a traditional Japanese company practicing "Japanese management." Even in Japan, Honda has long been considered a maverick.

And certainly the Marysville operation cannot be classified as traditional American management. It employs about 7,000 (and increasing rapidly) American "associates," and its managers are about half American and half Japanese.

If market success is the measure of leadership and an organization's culture, Honda is unquestionably a success. In the J. D. Powers & Associates survey of customer satisfaction in 1988, the Honda Acura was number one; the Honda Accord, manufactured in Marysville, was number two; Mercedes-Benz was number three. The three top-rated Imported Cars of the Year by *Motor Trend* magazine were all Honda Civics, among them the four-door Civic produced in Marysville. Honda has almost doubled U.S. production in the past year, and its cars are made of more American components (approaching 70 percent U.S.) than several models from Ford, General Motors, and Chrysler.

Honda is more than forty years old. Yet, as I found out visiting their operations, it possesses all of the qualities we would hope to find in our Synergistic company. Why is Honda so good? The answer is both simple and complex.

The executives and managers at Honda frequently discuss their philosophy, the values and visions upon which decisions and practices are based. Even before entering the building the philosophy became evident. As we drove toward the plant, I noticed lines of newly planted trees. I was told that they were planted by newly hired associates. Each new associate plants a tree "so they can grow with the company." All associates (the term used for all employees) know the company philosophy. They see it every day in a hundred ways. They hear it consistently from their leaders. There are no contradictions.

The president of Honda of America is Shoichiro Irimajiri, known as Mr. Iri by his associates. Earlier in his career, Mr. Iri was responsible for managing Honda's successful racing efforts, designing engines, and managing production facilities in Japan. He frequently speaks of the "racing spirit," which has five principles:

1. Seek the challenge.
2. Be ready on time.
3. Teamwork.
4. Quick response.
5. Winner takes all!

But perhaps more instructive of the Honda philosophy is a story he tells of one of his early racing efforts. In the 1965 British Grand Prix, an engine in a Formula 1 racing car designed by Mr. Iri failed. It was torn down and examined by Mr. Honda himself.

Finding that a faulty piston caused the problem, Mr. Honda demanded to know who had designed it.

"I did," said Shoichiro Irimajiri.

Mr. Honda then examined the piston's design specifications. "You! Stupid!" Honda roared. "No wonder the piston gets burned. You have changed the thickness."

After the young Irimajiri attempted to defend his design change with some data from previous engines, Mr. Honda roared again, "I hate college graduates! They use only their heads. Do you really think you can use obsolete data obtained from old, low-performance engines? I have been making and touching pistons for several tens of years. I am fully aware how critical half a millimeter is here. A company does not need people like you who use only their heads. Before you laid out this design, why didn't you listen to opinions of those experienced people in the shop? If you think academic study in college is everything, you are totally wrong. You will be useless in Honda unless you spend more time on the spot for many years to come.

"You will go to the machine shop," Mr. Honda ordered, "and apologize to every person there, for wasting their efforts." Mr. Honda followed him down the hall to make sure he did as directed.

Mr. Iri learned his lesson. He not only succeeded as an engineer, designing several successful racing engines, but he became the president of Honda of America, the first Japanese company to export cars back to Japan. Shoichiro Irimajiri is still listening to those experienced people in the shop, and he is not wasting their efforts. He has learned to appreciate specialized competence and to avoid the alienation induced by complex structure.

At Honda, engineers and management spend most of their time in the factory, in touch with their associates, the product, and the process. In traditional management there is a separation between "management" and the actual work. The line is impossible to find at Honda. Managers are working, literally, in the production line. They are studying, measuring, evaluating, not the people, but the product. No one appears to view his job as *checking up* or *controlling* the work of subordinates. They are hard on performance, but soft on people. Many less successful companies are hard on people, but soft on performance.

The Honda philosophy prevails throughout. In the structure, systems, skills, style, and symbols, the Synergistic philosophy can be seen and experienced every day, by every employee. Let's examine them one at a time.

Structure At Honda everyone is a member of a team, which is composed of fifteen to twenty associates who work in a common area. The team is the first level of organization, and it meets every morning at six-thirty. The day's work is discussed, and feedback on the previous day's quality is given. Any problems, changes, or concerns are shared during this meeting.

As I toured the Marysville motorcycle plant, I stood and watched the assembly line in operation. As I watched, one employee began to have difficulty getting a frame over a motorcyle engine. He had stopped the line. He and another associate worked frantically to get the frame in place. It took about twenty seconds, then the line was moving again. I asked where the team leader was. It turns out he was the associate who helped to free the frame. The team leader and production coordinator (equivalent of first-line supervisor and department manager) work on the line, smiling, joking, and working hard and fast with their fellow associates.

Nowhere is there a private office for team leaders or production coordinators. They are on the spot, seeing and touching the product, gaining experience, and solving problems. They are part of the working team. They can take immediate action, like the pit crew of Mr. Irimajiri's "racing spirit."

Just as employees work in teams, managers do too. Group problem solving is employed at every level of the organization. The structure of the organization, as well as the physical arrangement of desks and offices, makes group problem solving a natural and constant occurrence.

Participation in the constant improvement process is structured through Quality Circles. NH Circles (NH stands for "now Honda, new Honda, next Honda") are similar to circles in many other companies. However, at Honda they are just one component of a total involvement process that they call VIP (Voluntary Involvement Program). VIP includes a suggestion system, quality awards, and safety awards. Twenty percent of all associates participate in circles. In speaking with several NH Circle members, I was impressed that they felt the responsibility to see that accepted recommendations were implemented. They also felt that their circles are different from those in other companies because even small improvements are highly valued. They said that the success of Honda was the result of constantly finding small improvements, not just looking for major ones.

Systems I expected to find employee involvement at Marysville. However, I was surprised to see the amount of thought put into the positive reinforcement systems. There is constant feedback and tangible positive reinforcement for almost every form of desirable performance.

The NH Circle program, suggestion system, quality awards, and safety awards are all tied together with a point system, where by participating in the improvement process associates can earn a Honda Civic (2,500 points) or an Accord (5,000 points) plus two weeks off with pay and airplane tickets to anywhere in the world with spending money.

In addition to hourly or salaried compensation, all associates participate in profit sharing. This is an innovation of Honda of America and is not part of the system in Japan. Ten percent of gross profits are shared with associates based on their relative compensation. Good attendance results in another bonus. The average bonus check for attendance in 1986 was $832. The average profit-sharing check was $2,688.

Performance analysis and feedback is an important part of any performance management system. In each of the open office areas, and in each of the many conference rooms, the walls are covered with charts and graphs representing different quality and productivity performance variables. Frequently, alongside the charts are lists of causes or solutions to problems. Diagrams of auto parts or production machinery with arrows pointing to sources of problems are also frequent. It is obvious that all of the managers at Honda are in touch with plant performance data.

Another management technique worthy of mention is the discipline system. There are some fairly traditional and sound procedures for warnings, counseling, and discipline.

However, the unique part of the process is the peer review provided for associates who are dismissed for poor conduct. If an associate wishes to appeal a termination, a peer review panel is formed by randomly selecting six or eight production associates. One senior manager, with just one vote, also serves on the panel. The panel hears the case and then decides to overturn or accept management's decision. Nine out of ten times the decisions are upheld by the associates.

Skills Given the final product, there can be no question that Honda has highly skilled engineering and quality personnel. Because I have consulted with other auto companies, a major reason for this soon became obvious. Honda is an engineering company. The most valued personnel are those with engineering and technical competence. At many other companies it is the financial managers and management professionals who are held in high esteem. Honda is in the business of making excellent cars. Many other companies are in the business of making money and only secondarily make cars. Honda makes money and does not need layers of bureaucratic managers because it is passionately dedicated to its technology and products.

On the assembly line, there is a process of continual skill development. Associates are rotated to broaden their skills and increase their flexibility. Flexibility and the development of broad-based skills are central principles.

Honda's assembly process is based on just-in-time (JIT) inventory. There is only enough inventory maintained at the plant for one or two days' production. All suppliers understand that they must supply 100 percent good-quality parts in small quantities, "just in time" for the next day's production, or the plant will be shut down. This requires an intimate and cooperative relationship with all suppliers.

Each associate understands that it is his or her job to inspect each part to assure conformance to requirements. Any associate can reject a part. There is a quality assurance department with a team of associates who will call the supplier regarding every bad part. Every vendor is assigned to one associate, and that associate knows exactly whom to call and has the vendor's home telephone number.

The use of first-level associates in group decisions and exercising individual judgment assumes intelligence and competence. The assumption generally causes its development and realization. The cross-training of both production and managing associates builds an integrated, flexible base at every level of the organization.

Style All of the methods described above are held together by people with a sense of humor and a high level of people-to-people skills.

Every morning the ten or twelve Japanese and American managers of the motorcycle plant meet to review performance, solve problems, and make plans for the day. When I visited, the Japanese vice president responsible for the motorcycle operations sat at the end of the table. The meeting was led by a manager who was two levels down. There was a lively discussion about the handling of an "almost in time" inventory situation that had almost halted production the previous day. One of the Japanese managers was very vocal about how confused the situation was and how it should have been handled better. Several others discussed what happened and how it was being resolved. The vice president sat quietly through a half hour of discussion, saying nothing until the meeting was coming to a conclusion. Only then did he speak out. He had two points. First, he wanted to thank everyone for their efforts on the previous day. Second, he wanted to stress how important it was to meet another challenge that was coming up within the next week. His tone was calm and reassuring.

As I interviewed employees, I repeatedly asked them how they felt working for, or with, Japanese managers. I found absolutely no resentment, only the most sincere respect and friendship. There was no feeling of "us Americans" working for "them."

Symbols When I arrived I was given a uniform to wear in the plant. I was told that this wasn't given to everyone, only "honored guests." By the time my visit was finished, I felt honored. To be part of a proud group of people, to share their symbol of social cohesion, caused me to feel a part, invested, in their shared goals.

All employees, from the president to the newest hired associate, eat in the same cafeteria; park in the same undesignated parking spaces. Managers sit at the same metal desks in open office areas. Most of the desks are arranged in blocks of six, often with Japanese and American managers sitting across from one another. The absence of barriers, both physical and psychological, gives new meaning to the term *teamwork*.

As I walked through the plant, the cleanest nonfood manufacturing plant of several hundred I have been in, I observed a vice president stop and pick up a misplaced object on the floor. There is nothing on the floor. There are also *no* maintenance people to clean up! Everyone—every associate and manager—cleans his own area.

To many, these symbols will seem trivial. They would be if they stood alone, at odds with the behavior and attitudes of employees. However, symbols reinforce ideas, serve to create social unity.

Management at Honda is different from that at other Japanese companies, and this may be the key to their success in manufacturing in the United States. The traditional Japanese company places a high value on age and seniority. Honda does not. Mr. Honda has retired because he believes the company should be run by young men. Mr. Irimajiri is a young man excited by building high-performance racing engines and winning races. The first principle of the Honda management policy is "Proceed always with ambition and youthfulness." The second is "Respect sound theory, develop fresh ideas, and make the most effective use of time." The third is "Enjoy your work, and always brighten your working atmosphere."

As I left Marysville I didn't feel that I had visited a "foreign" manufacturer. Rather, I had the feeling that I had visited something new. I had seen a Synergistic, world-embracing company, as much American as Japanese, and perhaps the best of both worlds. I could also think of nothing Honda was doing that could not be adopted by any company—if its senior managers were knowledgeable, committed, and would "proceed always with youthfulness."

All cultures that succeed do so because of synergy, both within the culture and in interaction with competing cultures. Healthy companies are flexible. That allows them to change. Rigidity prevents change and inevitably leads to decline.

THE LAWS OF SYNERGY

There are nine axioms successful civilizations—and corporations—seem to follow to prevent that decline.

Axiom #1: Spirit

Corporations are both spiritual and material in nature. In their youth, they possess more spiritual than material assets. In decline this is reversed.

Corollary 1. It is the function of leaders to instill a unifying, challenging, and rewarding spirit.

Corollary 2. Health is maintained by unifying the spiritual and material assets. Leaders must appreciate the need for both.

Corollary 3. A decline in the spirit of a culture will precede and lead to a decline in material wealth.

Honda does not possess any unique material assets. There is little unique in technology. In fact, it is less automated than several other, less productive auto plants. Its competitive advantage is the same one Edison, Alexander, and Magellan had. It is the advantage of the human spirit.

In the last quarter of the twentieth century, our society has achieved material abundance and a relative condition of ease, conditions that—as we have seen—foster a loss of social purpose and internal division. Managers who view themselves as tough rigidly count and respond to the numbers. Rather than rallying the human spirit, they are quick to cut it down. To be truly tough is to rally one's subordinates to the fight, to inspire and lead the charge against uneven odds, rather than whine about unfair competition and undedicated subordinates. To be truly tough is to possess the spirit capable of inspiring others to raise their own standards and to overcome problems. But to accomplish all this requires a leader who, first, recognizes the power of the human spirit and, second, is in command of his own.

Axiom #2: Purpose

The purpose of a business is to create real wealth by serving its constituent groups—customers, stockholders, employees, and the general public.

Corollary 1. A group's performance is a result of common social purpose. It is the function of leadership to instill and reinforce social purpose.

Corollary 2. Emerging cultures possess a clear and unifying social purpose. In decline, that purpose is lost.

Corollary 3. The primary social purpose of a corporation is serving customers. All employees, at all levels, should know their customers and their needs.

Leaders create energy by instilling a sense of purpose. The manager is like the driver of the car, turning the wheel left and right, giving it direction and control. But the manager can turn the wheel all day and go nowhere if the engine is off or if there is no fuel in the tank.

The leader of the Synergistic corporation will realize he or she is in a position of service to his customers, employees, stockholders, and the general public. He will recognize that his own needs and rewards will come not by the direct pursuit of self-interest, but as a consequence of successfully serving the needs of others. He will also recognize his most powerful tool in motivating his followers is the creation of social unity through common purpose. There is no more important leadership task than motivation, and none for which managers are less trained and equipped.

The Synergist understands that motivation is derived from high self-esteem, which inevitably follows an understanding of one's purpose. This same understanding instills a willingness to sacrifice for the group. We feel better about ourselves, we feel noble, when we know that we have sacrificed for that which we hold to be noble.

And it is because of our search for our own nobility and self-esteem that we hope for leadership that will recognize the worthy cause and provide the opportunity to obtain the high self-esteem that comes from achieving it. For this reason, the corporate leader, like the Prophet, must explain what the worthy goal of the corporation is.

"God's own mad lover should die for the kiss, but not for thirty thousand dollars a year."
—JACK LONDON, *MARTIN EDEN*

This purpose must be stated not in financial terms, but in terms of being "the best"—the provider of the best-quality product or service. I realize this seems terribly routine, but it is critical. If you are coaching a football team, you begin every season with an eye on the championship, not on achieving an "average" performance. There is little satisfaction in achieving the average, whether in sports or business. It is striving for the best that creates excitement and sacrifice, nothing less.

All senior managers must be able to talk about this purpose in a way that leaves no room for confusion among subordinates. Unfortunately, within many corporations the only consistency in purpose is that the mission is constantly being redefined and restudied. This —quite clearly—sends the message to employees that the senior managers do not know what the company is dedicated to. It is a sorry fact that most corporate executives are not dedicated to any mission.

The organization's mission must be stated in a manner that can be understood by the first-level employee. Because managers in a Bureaucratic organization have so little empathy for employees, they often state it in terms of return on assets, percentage of annual growth, and so forth. This has absolutely no meaning to employees. These are not the terms that the Prophet used. He spoke in terms they understood. "To make the best car in the world." "To provide the highest-quality health care in the world at a price the average person can afford." Sure, these are simple. But they are clear and easily understood.

Axiom #3: Creativity

Business's most important job is to create new and improved products, services, and means of production.

    Corollary 1. Leadership must be creative to stimulate creativity.

    Corollary 2. Change, youthfulness, and energy are requirements until death.

    Corollary 3. Flexibility, challenge, the free and frank flow of ideas and information, are necessary to promote creativity.

From our analysis of life cycles we know facing challenges, and responding creatively to those challenges, are the prerequisites of growth. Organizations remain healthy when the leaders are creative. Once leaders start to rely on responses that were successful in the past, failure results in the presence of new challenge. We have also learned that large and specialized organizations require increasing administration, yet administrations tend to block creativity.

To maintain synergy, the leader must be aware of this very delicate balance between the preservation of creativity and the need for order. It is one of the most significant challenges in the mature period of a corporation's life and demands a creative response. It also demands flexibility. Those who lean toward creativity will be required to sacrifice for the sake of administrative sanity. Those on the other end will have to sacrifice the perfection of complete accounting and reporting procedures. There will have to be a recognition that some disorder is a sign of growth and vitality. There also will have to be the contrary recognition that complete disorder leads to disaster. The perfect balance will never be found, and the Synergist will constantly listen to arguments for moving the fulcrum one way or the other.

How do leaders remain creative? By staying in touch with their customers and employees. Why? Because this is the arena of business challenges. This is where constant growth and learning are required in order to remain competitive. And only those who are growing and learning can be creative. Leaders lose their creativity when they become consumed by administration, finance, and external affairs that take them away from the real work.

I propose that there be a rule within each company that every manager, including the CEO, spend at least *one-half* of his time dealing with matters directly related to producing and selling.

Many managers have responded to the call in *In Search of Excellence* for "MBWA," management by walking around. This is great, except some managers have misunderstood the key point. They think the purpose of this wandering is merely to be seen and to mix with the common man. But that is not the way it worked when MBWA was created at Hewlett-Packard. John Young walked around so that he could give advice and also because he was genuinely interested in what was going on. He was able to call on what he learned in his wanderings when it came time to make a decision.

Axiom #4: Challenge and Response

The task of leaders is to create or recognize the current challenge, respond creatively, and avoid a condition of ease.

Corollary 1. Effort is the result of perceived challenge and anticipated successful response.

Corollary 2. Reliance on yesterday's successful response in the face of new challenge leads to decline.

Corollary 3. Recognizing and responding to challenges requires a culture that is dynamic, never static.

It is ironic that satisfaction and security are the enemies of excellence. I have never met an excellent manager who was satisfied. Every excellent manager—or artist, writer, engineer, or scientist, for that matter—I have met always had another, higher goal in mind as they neared the one they had set earlier. They constantly provided their own motivations—and challenges.

The Synergist has a finely tuned ear to the motivational pulse beat of his organization. He never allows security or satisfaction to lull his crew to sleep at the wheel. He knows his job is to establish the challenge that excites the thoughts and creates energy that demands action. He knows he can only achieve urgency in others if he possesses that same urgency himself.

The Synergist also knows that he must create within each employee the belief in his own ability to determine his fate. If an employee doesn't have that faith, he will talk for hours about things he can't control: the economy, unions, foreign competition, government, the press, and the misbehavior of customers and suppliers. With all those things going against him, anyone would fail!

In the Synergistic organization every member believes he can exert his will and help determine the organization's future. He believes this because his leader does. In his decisions and everyday conversations, the leader communicates his positive outlook on the future. He cannot succeed with some false effort at selling a belief that he does not truly hold. While lip service is common today in our organizations, it almost never works. Employees are sensitive to the messages they receive. Most possess surefire, automatic crap detectors.

Axiom #5: Planned Urgency

The urgency to decide and act promptly leads to expansion and advance. Prompt action must be balanced by deliberate planning.

Corollary 1. Planning that results in late action is useless.

Corollary 2. Action that does not serve long-term interests is useless.

Corollary 3. There will always be conflict between promptness and planning.

During a company's early states, there are lots of quick decisions and little careful planning. As the company declines, the opposite is true. Entrepreneurs succeed because they move more quickly than slow, defensive, large organizations. The speed of decision making is based on the balance between risk and opportunity. Unnecessary risks are to be avoided, but so are lost opportunities. And the Synergist is constantly trying to keep his organization balanced between the two. He constantly tries to ensure decisions are well thought through, and that decisions with greater cost and more strategic impact are subject to greater analysis. But the Synergist is also a "get it done now" kind of manager. Once a decision is made he demands quick action to capitalize on the benefits of decision.

The tension between urgency and planning is a constant strain in companies such as IBM, where the external market moves quickly. The sheer size of IBM makes mobilization difficult. As a result, IBM has frequently been outmaneuvered, whether in the personal computer field by Apple and Compaq, in the midsize computers by DEC, or in the supercomputers by Cray Research. For many years IBM succeeded in moving quickly despite its mass. In recent years, however, as the market has begun to move ever faster, the giant appears too slow, losing business to the host of faster-moving Barbarians.

Entrepreneurial ventures are rarely accused of excessive planning. And that is probably good. If they planned carefully, many never would have set off on the journey of building a new enterprise. Starting a new business is daunting enough without a computer printout telling you why it cannot be done.

All planning is based on predictions about the external environment. If there is war in the Persian Gulf, all of the most careful plans of the oil companies go up in smoke. Even for the largest multinational firms, the need to move quickly in response to external events is a more significant factor in success than careful planning. Here is the tension of planning and urgency. The large firm with huge investments has a responsibility to carefully weigh options and implications of major decisions. On the other hand, it must be willing to abandon or alter those plans on short notice.

Axiom #6: Unity and Diversity

Advancing cultures become diverse in character. Leaders must act to unify diverse talents and traits.

Corollary 1. Leaders must actively resist the tendency to attract and promote like personalities and skills.

Corollary 2. The highest-quality decisions are attained through consensus. Consensus is most valuable when it represents the collective wisdom of participants with diverse views and experience.

As we have seen throughout, successful corporations understand they need diverse personalities to succeed. The Synergist raises this understanding to a new level. He not only tolerates diversity, he genuinely appreciates it. He transcends his own management style and encourages and supports capable people with very different points of view.

There can be little doubt that hamburger king Ray Kroc, a Barbarian/Explorer, was also a Synergist. He appreciated the necessary differences among his subordinates. "If a corporation has two executives who think alike, one of them is unnecessary," Kroc is reported to have said.

To this day, McDonald's is probably the only major corporation with a vice president for individuality. Jim Kuhn was given this position and charged with developing incentives and programs to foster individual initiative. Chairman Fred Turner proudly points out that many of the marketing initiatives and most of the product development have come not from the corporate planning departments, but from the individual franchisees. Though the McDonald's system may appear regimented from the outside, Turner points out that

> The independent-mindedness of our operators prevents regimentation. While they stick to the basics of the system, they zig and zag by making refinements and changes, and everyone benefits from their willingness to zig and zag. The system deals with setting uniform standards, but regimentation? No way.[1]

The genius of Ray Kroc was not in perfecting hamburgers, corporate strategy, financial management, or even motivating people. It was in creating a culture that continues to foster creativity and an aggressive commitment to its market. Ray Kroc loved hamburgers, and McDonald's still does, rejecting numerous proposals for mergers or opportunities to enter into the theme park, motel, or other business. Strong and diverse personalities dedicated to a single mission has been the key to McDonald's success.

In his excellent book on McDonald's, John Love points out:

> Kroc was an intensely emotional man with extremely strong opinions on how things should work and how people should behave. He was a man with uncompromising old-world values. His judgments on issues and people were black and white. But . . . as he put together his first group of corporate managers, he suppressed his strong likes and dislikes of personal traits in order to pick and promote people for their skills. Even when their

personal habits drove him up a wall, he found ways of venting his anger in order to keep talented people.[2]

June Martino was his secretary through his entire career, rising to become secretary and treasurer of the corporation and a member of the board of directors. Her primary skills, however, were not secretarial or even financial; they were interpersonal. She was the communicator, mediator, and the one who preserved family unity.

Harry Sonneborn was Ray Kroc's closest partner in the founding of the McDonald's corporation. Yet in personality and talents, he was Kroc's opposite. Kroc was the outgoing salesman. Sonneborn was the introvert who was often regarded as cold, impersonal, and secretive. Kroc enjoyed being out in the stores where the action was. Sonneborn enjoyed managing the company by the numbers and liked the prestige of being with the company's lawyers and bankers. Kroc took pride in making millionaires out of the independent franchises. Sonneborn took pride in the return to investors and the company's growing strength in New York financial circles. Here was a Barbarian/Explorer who had made an Administrator his closest associate.

Ray Kroc recognized and appreciated these differences.

I didn't give a damn about money, and I didn't pay as much attention to that part of the business as I should have. All I wanted was a winner in the hamburger business, and I sort of took profits for granted. But Harry didn't know or care a damn thing about hamburgers and french fries. When it came to what the company sold and who the franchisees were, Harry was far away from it. He was a cold, calculating money man, but I needed a guy like that.[3]

Fred Turner, another early employee, perhaps did more than anyone else to develop the systems that would realize Ray Kroc's vision of quality, cleanliness, and service. Turner was a college dropout who took a job working as an assistant manager in a Mc-

Donald's in the Chicago area at a salary of $100 a week. Kroc was impressed with Turner's intensity and asked him to train new franchisees. Within months Turner was defining virtually all operating procedures, writing manuals for franchisees to follow, and developing the industry's best system for monitoring and grading the performance of the stores. Turner was the Builder who did for store operations what Sonneborn had done for the company's finances.

After Kroc bought out Sonneborn, Turner became president. His style allowed McDonald's to make a successful transition into maturity while maintaining its creativity and energy.

Turner was a Synergist who, like Kroc, recognized the need to balance a diversity of management styles. But unlike Kroc, Turner's personality was more naturally balanced, less prone to emotional outbursts. Turner began creating one of the most decentralized decision-making processes in corporate America. He recognized that in a business where the production and service functions were themselves highly decentralized, greater quality control could be achieved by decentralizing decision making.

Turner's tendency toward synergy was also evident in his dealings with his new chief financial officer, Dick Boylan, a Sonneborn protégé who felt that he should have gotten the top job. Turner appreciated Boylan's financial skills and allowed him to fully manage McDonald's financial affairs. Boylan and Turner developed a close partnership, much to the surprise of many who expected competition between the two men.

McDonald's success is clearly the result of different personalities leading the corporation at different stages of its development. It is a classic example of synergy.

How does the Synergist unify people with diverse styles, talents, backgrounds, education, and experience? There is only one way, and it is the Synergist's innovation. He develops a culture that embraces diversity.

The Synergist knows he is like the orchestra conductor who has percussionists who love to pound away at the drums and violinists who caress their instruments. He knows if they were all the same, they could not possibly make orchestral music. Or he is like the tender of a rose garden, who knows it would be a dull garden indeed if all the roses were the same color. It is in the very differences, the contrasts of color and sound, that beauty is to be found.

One manager or employee might be a brilliant engineer enraptured by hardware and another a lover of talk who could sell the Brooklyn Bridge. The Synergist finds this diversity pleasing, not frustrating. He knows he would be less successful, less of a leader, and less capable of creative responses if all the members of his team were suited to play the same position. This attitude of genuine appreciation, rather than tolerance, is one of the critical signs of the Synergist. It is the breakthrough that terminates internal warfare within the organization. The problem with the warfare is that if both sides battle to a draw, nothing gets done. And if one side wins—say the Administrators over the Builders—there are less resources to draw upon.

But it is hard to tolerate this diversity. The easiest team to manage is comprised of clones, all thinking alike, behaving alike, with the same backgrounds and experience. It is one of our less fortunate characteristics that we seek ease. We therefore seek out other managers and employees who are similar to us. In so doing we rob ourselves of the differences of background, experience, and ideas that will enrich us. We also rob the organization of creativity. Diversity is an extremely valuable corporate asset.

> Is uniformity of opinion attainable? Millions of innocent men, women, and children, since the introduction of Christianity, have been burnt, tortured, fined, imprisoned; yet we have not advanced one inch toward uniformity. What has been the effect of coercion? to make one half the world fools, and the other half hypocrites.
>
> —THOMAS JEFFERSON

Axiom #7: Specialized Competence

Specialized knowledge and skills must be pursued vigorously. Once obtained, the skills must be integrated.

Corollary 1. Efficient methods are derived from specialized competence; however, specialized competence can lead to inefficient methods.

Corollary 2. The highest technical competence leads to competitive advantage, *if* put to the service of customers, both internal and external.

Corollary 3. Employees at all levels should work in small groups or teams toward a common purpose, as an integrating mechanism.

When organizations are born there is little specialization. As they grow, specialization is inevitable. Salespersons will be highly trained; a production worker in one corner of the plant will be highly skilled on one piece of equipment but may have little knowledge of another one hundred feet away.

With specialization there is the increasing danger of social disintegration. A worker no longer understands how everything fits together, why what he does helps or hinders the work of someone else, and how his work ultimately affects the customer. And as the company grows more specialized, no one is willing to take responsibility when something goes wrong. For example, personnel managers hire new employees, so the first-line supervisor, who complains about the incompetence of the new employee, accepts little responsibility for the employee's training and success.

The work of the Synergist is to create effective integration of these specialists. It won't be easy. A major reason for poor-quality goods and services is the failure of integration. Separate groups of design engineers and manufacturing engineers, both brilliant in their fields, fail to work together. The result is a poor-quality car because the manufacturing process was not considered in the design.

I recently completed work with Moody's Investor Services, which publishes investor manuals. My associates and I redesigned the total organization system around principles of integration and involvement.

In the old system, new employees were hired by a manager to sit at a computer terminal and input a specialized, narrow set of data. They were only responsible for their own work.

In the new system employees are hired by the members of the

first-level team on which they will serve. That team is responsible for delivering a product to a customer, making decisions about the methods of production, analyzing problems, and finding ways to continually improve quality and performance. All team members have the opportunity to learn all aspects of the job. This provides flexibility. Team members can help each other, check each other's work, and assist in problem solving. The work is integrated. As a result production has increased drastically, and innovations in both new products and product improvements have resulted. It is also more fun to work there!

The Synergist achieves both vertical as well as horizontal integration. In the declining corporation the levels become detached from each other. The more layers there are in an organization, the worse the communication from top to bottom—and the more difficult it is for people at the top to understand the productive work. Excessive layers kill motivation and creativity. You can almost draw a direct negative correlation between the numbers of layers in an organization and the motivation of the employees.

The Synergistic organization does not require as many layers because the common social purpose drives, not controls.

Axiom #8: Efficient Administration

As differentiation increases, efficient administration is required to achieve integration and performance.

Corollary 1. The greater the differentiation in an organization, the greater the need for administration.

Corollary 2. The weight of administration tends to grow unless deliberately checked by leadership.

Corollary 3. Unchecked administration inevitably leads to bureaucracy and the decline of creativity and wealth creation.

The original purpose of administration was first, to provide for the integration and coordination of diverse elements within the organization, and second, to serve the operations by providing scorekeeping mechanisms. In periods of decline, that purpose becomes lost.

The Synergist understands the purpose of administration. He knows systems and structure were designed to serve customers. He makes sure they do so. Consider Springfield Remanufacturing Center Corp.

In 1983 John P. Stack and twelve other employees purchased SRC in a leveraged buy-out from International Harvester Company. SRC was then losing $2 million a year on sales of $26 million. Since the leveraged buy-out, SRC's sales have grown 40 percent per year; net operating income rose 11 percent; the debt-to-equity ratio has been cut from 89-to-1 to 5-to-1; and the appraised value of the stock has increased from $.10 to $8.45. At the same time absenteeism and employee turnover, once high, have virtually disappeared.

The turnaround is almost entirely the result of new administrative processes designed to improve performance by increasing commitment, rather than control. This little backwoods company of a few hundred folks in Springfield, Missouri, has developed a financial reporting system that does more to improve performance than any developed by the biggest and allegedly most sophisticated *Fortune* 500 companies. The SRC system should be copied by the big guys!

The SRC system is entirely based on numbers, but they are numbers shared with everyone. The numbers allow every employee to track how well they—and the company—are doing. Says Stack:

> When you walk through this factory you hear numbers everywhere you go. It's like you're in the middle of a bingo tournament. I just felt that, if you were going to spend a majority of your time doing a job, why couldn't you have fun at it? For me, fun was action, excitement, a good game. If there's one thing common to everybody, it's that we love to play a good game.[4]

Stack believes that business is essentially a game and everyone can learn to play. There are classes for every manager and employee in how to read SRC's profit-and-loss and income statements. Every employee sees those numbers daily, weekly, and monthly. Every employee discusses them—in the most frank terms—within his team led by a supervisor. By sharing this information, each employee learns what he has to do to make the company successful. This is the key to the system.

"Watching this organization is like watching a continuous Dow Jones ticker tape. Literally. In the cafeteria, there is a flashing electronic board reporting the performance of one department for that very morning based on their labor utilization rate," says Stack. As one employee said: "Before, I wasn't in a thinking mood, but now you know you're helping yourself as well as the company." Every employee can earn bonuses and profit sharing based on the company's success.

The constant flow of financial numbers to each work area has put everyone in "a thinking mood." Or, as another SRC manager said: "What happened here is that now these people are in effect running their own small businesses. They set their own budgets, and they have to live with them. If they want to complain, they have to complain to themselves. This is above all an awareness program. Every little bit counts, and only the people here can make the numbers work."

SRC went from an unhappy ugly duckling, unappreciated in the large bureaucracy of a declining company, to a lovely swan. There was a complete transformation in culture. The leaders were able to instill a common social purpose within the organization. The administrative systems were used as they should be: to integrate the work of different elements and to motivate performance.

In the Synergistic company all employees are served by the administrative process. The immediate attention to numbers, and their use as a team scoreboard, can produce social integration. They must, however, be used positively, for winning and celebrating rather than for controlling. This is efficient administration.

Axiom #9: On-the-Spot Decisions

Decisions should be made by those on the spot, close to the customer, product, or service. The farther decisions are removed from the point of action, the worse the quality and the higher the cost.

Corollary 1. In the youthful company, decision makers are on the spot and in direct contact with customers, products, or service. In decline they are not.

Corollary 2. Command decision making is employed in stages of immaturity and extreme decay. Consensus is a sign of maturity and health.

Corollary 3. Internal conflict results in increased control, control produces fear, and fear drives decisions up the organization and drives out creativity.

Command leadership is appropriate during the corporation's earliest days. But that was then, this is now, and the corporation is far from young. The Synergist has a high level of respect for his subordinates and peers. He recognizes that he will be most successful if he calls upon their collective wisdom in making important decisions. The Synergist recognizes the need for different styles of decision making. He knows that less important, short-term decisions are best made unilaterally or in consultation with one or two team members. He does not waste the team's time with issues that are only of concern to a few members. But he knows that there is a time to call two or three of his subordinates together for quick conferences, and he knows that issues such as group goals and corporate management practices are worth the investment of the entire team's collaboration.

TEAMWORK

In Synergistic organizations, managers at every level of the organization view themselves as team leaders who are skilled at leading group problem-solving sessions that maximize the collaboration across units of the organization. These meetings provide a forum in which these managers are educated in the problems and concerns of other departments.

The nine most senior managers of Delta Airlines constitute what I would describe as a Synergistic team. Every Monday morning they meet to discuss major issues facing the company, to report any major events in each of their areas, and to get advice from other team members. It is this last feature that is most important. It is this willingness to seek advice that genuinely makes this a Synergistic company.

The culture of Delta Airlines is the result neither of any short-term effort nor any specific program. It is the result of consistent management practices, beliefs, and behavior, from top to bottom. The "Delta family feeling" begins with the family feeling among the nine senior executives who have the maturity to talk together as adults, who look to learn from each other. It is this feeling of respect and maturity that provides the basis for the Synergistic teams.

In his book, *Seven Habits of Highly Successful People,* Stephen R. Covey has described three stages of maturity:

> **Dependence:** the infant's total dependence on the parent.
> **Independence:** the adolescent breaking away to establish his or her own identity separate and apart from parents.
> **Interdependence:** the stage where one is confident enough to make the sacrifice to another, to enter into a collaborative relationship, such as marriage and family.[5]

Organizations go through similar stages of development. The Synergist has reached the maturity of interdependence, able to rely on and collaborate with others. He is willing to delegate decisions to those who are the true experts: the people in touch with customers, products, and service.

THE COMING GLOBAL SYNERGY

When dominant civilizations and corporations become geographically dispersed and complex, they take one of two paths in order to maintain control of their empires. They either develop rigid and bureaucratic structures or they enter a period of internal synergy.

The first course inevitably leads to rebellion and internal war-fare.

The second course allows them to achieve higher levels of integration and continue their dominance and development. This can be seen in the development of the United States and in the present challenge of world order.

The Founding Fathers recognized the unique challenge with which they were confronted and responded with a creativity that is unique in history. Those who met in Philadelphia two hundred years ago possessed both vision and the courage to take decisive action. They developed a synergy among states to form a nation. They rejected the conservative response: clinging to the provincial structure of sovereign states. They recognized that the increased size, complexity, and interdependence of the growing society called for higher levels of integration. That integration became the United States.

The growth of the global economic system, with its increasing size, complexity, and interdependence, requires integration and synergy. We are entering a period of one world civilization. All of the factors that once defined the boundaries of civilization now define a global culture. Instant global communications have shrunk physical distance. Shared cultural metaphors and experience—from Michael Jackson T-shirts in Tibetan villages to Paul Simon's *Graceland* album, which incorporated African tribal rhythms—shows that the pulse of the world is gradually moving toward the same beat.

If our present leaders are endowed with creative vitality, they will recognize that our world situation is very similar to that faced by America's Founding Fathers two hundred years ago. We can only hope they respond creatively.

Managing Competitive Strategy Within

T he corporate executive, like the leader of a nation, must have both an internal (domestic) and external (foreign) policy. Both need to be strong, but in the corporation that is rarely the case. Executives generally devote most of their resources to external policy, exploring new markets, products, growth rates, and competition. They tend to concentrate less on internal policies, where they must answer the question "What kind of society do we want to have in this organization?" They need to pay more attention to the internal strategy, their vision of their future society.

In the last chapter I described that almost utopian organization, the Synergistic one, at the top of the life cycle curve. In this chapter I will describe a framework to assess and move toward synergy.

Most of my career has been spent working within corporations helping them change. It is messy work. It always involves conflict, since changing the corporate culture means changing the habits of the people who make up the organization. And habits, of course, are hard to change.

It is for precisely this reason that the culture of an organization represents a competitive advantage or disadvantage. In days past, property, capital, or technology were significant elements in competitive advantage. But today all of those factors are easily transferred from one organization to another, hence lessening the advantage. The culture, the habits of the people, are not so easily transferred, however. The culture of Honda, IBM, or Delta is not easily created in either a young emerging company or an old declining company. That in large part is what gives these companies their competitive edge.

ORGANIZED THINKING—THE FOUNDATION OF SYSTEMATIC ACTION

Perhaps it is too obvious to say that progress is impossible without a conceptual framework. However, despite all the talk of recent years, most managers are attacking the issue of corporate culture without one. This has resulted in actions that appear disjointed and frantic.

A company's culture is the sum of the habits of its members. Simply put, it is the "normal way we get things done around here." More comprehensively, it is the structure, systems, skills, style, and symbols that reflect the core values and visions of its members and are affected by the external forces (social, political, economic, and technological) of the environment. The culture changes constantly. Those changes follow a predictable pattern that is the life cycle curve.

There is no one right way to evaluate a culture. However, the following model has proven successful in helping managers evaluate and plan the culture of their organization. We begin with a question: What kind of a culture, what kind of minisociety, do we want for our organization? This is the most important question that the leaders of every organization must be able to answer.

THE ABILITY TO CREATE WEALTH

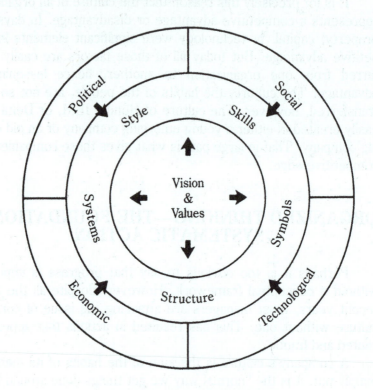

VALUES AND VISIONS:
THE HEART AND MIND

To manage or change an organization's culture, a leader must first define its visions and values. Intuitively, all great leaders have understood that their power was built upon the vision they shared with their followers. When President John F. Kennedy called upon people to "ask not what your country can do for you, but what you can do for your country," he was calling for sacrifice toward a common vision.

The vision and values of a company are often captured in simple phrases. At Delta Airlines it is the "Delta family feeling." At Dun & Bradstreet, "customer focus." At Honda Manufacturing it is "the Honda way" and "the racing spirit." Simple statements all. Yet behind those statements are legends, emotions, and subtleties that affect the decisions of employees every day. The slogans are a shorthand way of expressing the company's vision, and it is that vision which gives these companies their competitive advantage.

Consider Eastern and Delta airlines. At seminars and speaking engagements during the last several years I have asked audiences whether they knew the name of the former or present chief executive of Eastern Airlines. They all knew either Frank Borman or Frank Lorenzo. I then asked if they knew the CEO of Delta. Virtually no one did. I then asked which airline would they prefer to fly? Almost everyone said Delta. I then asked which airline stock they'd own. Again, the choice was Delta. It is significant that few people know who David Garrett is. At Delta it is not the chairman who is important. Every employee is. This is the basis of the "Delta family feeling."

That feeling has a long history and genuinely affects the thoughts, feelings, and behavior of every employee. The feeling begins at the top, where the nine senior executives meet every Monday morning. Unlike most management meetings, which are little more than one-on-one reporting in a forum for public humiliation, Delta's is a genuine working session. This feeling of teamwork at the top affects the way these executives treat their subordinates and cascades down through the organization all the way to the flight attendants, who treat their customers well because they have been treated well. It is not hard to understand.

I consulted with Ford Motor Company in the late 1970s, before it began its revitalization now so apparent. When I interviewed managers, I asked whom their role models were. One executive told me about his early "boss," who, unlike the current crop of weaker managers, knew how to "take care of the union." He recalled the famed "Battle of the Overpass" when union leaders were met on the bridge at the Rouge River plant by thugs and were brutally beaten and thrown off the bridge. Incredibly, this manager recalled the incident as an example of management when it was strong, in control. I could tell by the determined look in his eyes that he was most sincere in his longing for those "good old days." I asked several managers who reported similar values if they had any other models or heroes who were still active at Ford. They could not think of any. Their values and visions of management lay in the ashes of a violent past.

The people of primitive or declining cultures worship heroes of the past—their dead ancestors. Cultures that are growing and vital have heroes of the present. At Ford, the people who worship the past are now gone from leadership positions. The current leaders love their product. They are former engineers and men who enjoy driving race cars. They know, firsthand, the character of a quality car. They are the heroes of the present. The slogan "At Ford, Quality Is Job One" was designed to focus all members of the organization—managers and employees—on quality. The leaders of Ford have struggled to instill the value of quality and the vision of Ford as the highest-quality car maker. This is something all employees can embrace.

To ensure they do, teamwork between management and labor at Ford has become unprecedented in the U.S. auto industry. Ford's leaders have created social unity through common purpose. If a company is to be known for the quality of its products or services, it will be because the leaders have established the value and vision of quality leadership.

When Lee Iacocca took over as chief executive at Chrysler, he did not begin trying to save the company by instituting new administrative procedures. He began by preaching. He understood he had inherited a corpse that needed to be reborn, not only materially, but spiritually. The managers and employees of Chrysler needed faith, belief in the possibilities of the future. No organization can create its own future if its members lack a positive vision. Iacocca went on television not only to sell the public cars, but to sell his employees on the future.

Perhaps these may seem small events. But without them no administrative procedures will truly work. Before a company can succeed, there must be a foundation that allows creative energy, dedication, and sacrificial effort, all stemming from a vision of the future.

How can a manager create a unifying vision in his company? There are four specific things he can do.

1. Develop a Vision Statement The organization's leaders must agree on what the company should become. This shared vision is the common religion, ethic, and guide to the organization's future. In an emerging company the management team may not have the maturity to develop such a vision. In that case the leader, the Prophet/Barbarian, must declare it. This statement should include both the external vision (future markets, products, or services) and the internal culture.

2. Sell the Vision A written statement printed in the corporate newsletter, read at the annual conference, or pasted on the wall does not sell. The vision must be marketed. It must be presented over and over again, like an advertising campaign introducing a new product. Selling the vision is never a one-time thing; it requires continual communication.

Employees do listen. Unfortunately they often hear too well. The executive promotes an idea in one speech but forgets it in the next. The employees then forget, too. The senior executives should refer to the vision in literally every talk they give to managers and employees. Constant reminders and restatement of the vision is essential if it is to become part of the culture.

3. Make the Vision an Active Reference Point When managers are making significant decisions, they should refer to the vision statement and ask whether their decision is furthering or detracting from the vision. For example, your vision may include the idea that every employee must be involved in making decisions and accept responsibility for his work. You are now considering a training program for new employees. Does the program help employees make decisions about their own work?

The question you should ask every time is, Is this decision consistent with the company's vision? If it isn't, don't make it.

4. Praise and Publicize Models Values become clear when behavior consistent with those values is praised and publicized. Write down the two, three, or four key values that are important in your company. In your last talk to managers or employees, did you talk about staff members who exhibited those values? If you don't praise people for living up to the company's values, it will be assumed those values are not very important. When executives of 3M speak to employees, they will almost always refer to internal examples of innovation. When David Kearns, CEO of Xerox, speaks to the staff employees, he almost always talks about the importance of quality improvement and education. When Alexander the Great spoke to his troops, he always spoke of bravery and sacrifice in battle. Do you stress what is important?

THE FIVE S'S: THE BODY OF THE CULTURE

Managers must translate beliefs into action. After all, it is action that produces results. Values are expressed throughout the organization as management creates structure, systems, skills, style, and symbols. If values and vision are the heart and mind of the culture, these five S's are the body.

Structure

I began my career working as a counselor in the North Carolina Department of Corrections. Perhaps nowhere is the power of an organization's structure more obvious than in a prison.

In the early 1970s there was a university study designed to determine the effects of prison structure on human behavior. A mock prison was devised, and twenty graduate students in psychology, products of a humanistic liberal education, were randomly divided into two groups: inmates and guards. For ten days, twenty-four hours a day, the students lived the life of inmates and guards. Unfortunately, the experiment had to end early. Why? Because the inmates were being physically abused by the guards. The inmates, after only a few days, had resorted to plotting against the guards and taunting them. The guards responded out of frustration. After the experiment was called off, the students and professor sat together to talk about their experience; none of them could understand their own behavior. The environment, role, and structure of this mock prison had exerted an influence that overcame the education and humanistic values of these students. The roles and structure of corporations accomplish the same.

Just as the role definitions imposed by the prison structure influenced the behavior of these psychology students, the structure of management-union, supervisor-worker, and salaried-hourly relationships constantly influence the thinking and behavior of employees.

Frito-Lay, Sherwin-Williams, Best Foods, Moody's Investor Services, and many other companies have changed their structure based on visions of a new culture. In each case, layers of management have been reduced by moving decision making into the work force. The Dana Corporation has one plant in which there is a shift with only one manager for over 250 employees. Obviously the assumptions about organizational structure are significantly different from those in a traditional organization. It represents a new vision of the role of employees.

Companies that remain Synergistic do so by keeping workers in touch with decision making and leaders in touch with the work. The traditional corporate structure has been built on the assumption that it is the manager's job to define, measure, and control the work of employees and that employees could not make significant decisions regarding their own work. The primary value was control, not commitment or creativity. Upon this value Max Weber built his theory of organization and Frederick Taylor created his principles of "scientific management," which laid the foundation for most traditional organizational structure. The average span of control—that is, the number of employees reporting to a manager—at the first level of U.S. manufacturing companies today is seven, *exactly what it was one hundred years ago.*

Why is 1-to-7 the right span of control? Why not 1-to-20 or 1-to-30? The manager will reply, "How can I control the work of thirty employees?"

Perhaps you can't. But they can control their own work.

The average span of control in Japanese chemical companies is more than 1:20; at similar U.S. plants it is 1:8.

Employees aren't the greatest cause of corporate inefficiency. Managers are, by assuming they must "control" employees, check every action, and control the checkers with more checkers. Until recently, Ford had sixteen layers, compared with six at Toyota, yet Ford's quality and employee efficiency were worse, a fact that Ford recognized. The company has now substantially reduced layers of management and increased spans of control by giving employees more say in their jobs. The result has been a substantial improvement in both output per employee and quality.

The culture of Dana Corporation has been revolutionized, as management has been reduced from fifteen layers to five. Xerox has reduced layers in its manufacturing and service organizations, while at the same time increasing market share, quality, and customer service ratings. There is more and more evidence that the greater the number of management layers, the less efficient employee productivity. In other words, there is an inverse relationship between the amount of management control and the resulting quality in either product or service.

The structure of the organization is an obvious way of seeing what management believes. The structure of the Catholic church, the Roman legions, and the British bureaucracy all reflect the values of those who created them. Structure and behavior are constantly interacting to form the fabric of the minisociety we call a corporation.

Action Plans to Improve Structure

1. Redesign the Organization Institute a planning process by which your managers and employees may redesign the organization. A steering committee of senior managers should write a charter to define the principles, or vision, upon which the structure should be built. Design teams made up of line managers and employees must then be trained and led through a process where they consider work flow and all matters relating to the organization. Their task is to create the ideal future structure. Their recommendations are then presented to the steering committee for approval.

I believe this process, which relies on the intelligence and commitment of employees and managers, rather than on external "experts," is the best way to change a department or business.

2. Track Spans of Control I am amazed how few managers are aware of the numbers of layers of management and spans of control they have created. Once you understand the relationship between competitive advantage and the structure of the organization, it then makes sense to keep precise data on that structure, especially the numbers of layers and spans of control.

There can be no simple rules for the numbers of layers or the span of control. They will vary with the work. Obviously, a factory in which repetitive work is the norm can have larger work units than a high-tech engineering department in which first-level managers are heavily involved in problem solving. However, a study of competitors can provide direction and the basis for quantifiable goals. Du Pont, for example, studied competing chemical plants in the United States, Europe, and Japan before establishing the goal of substantially increasing their spans of control. This effort produced substantial savings without hindering operational effectiveness.

3. Define the Existing Organization into Teams You may not be prepared to totally redesign your organization. Still, you can reduce management layers and give employees more of a say in their jobs. Here's one way: rather than thinking about your organization chart as a series of one-on-one reporting relationships, think of it as a series of interlocking triangles, where the organization is comprised of managers and employees, working in teams, where each team is led by a senior person who is a member of the team above.

This team organization requires no revolution in structure— only changes in skills and style. It implies that the leader of each team is the facilitator of problem solving and decision making within the group. It assumes managers will encourage team members to take responsibility for their own performance. If the manager begins to act more as a team leader, the members will begin to act more as managers. Over time this thinking reduces the need for increasing structure and reduces alienation. This process has been successful at Tennessee Eastman, Metropolitan Life Insurance Company, Southwestern Bell, and other companies.

Systems

The flow of information, performance appraisal, and systems of promotion and compensation are among the dozens of systems that allow the organization to maintain efficiency and sanity. Without systems, every event would be treated as unique and require a separate judgment. Chaos would result.

But exactly what "order" is it that the systems are maintaining? The information flow of the military organization causes all information to flow upward to the commanding officer, with little, if any, horizontal flow. That makes sense on the battlefield, where the commanding officers make the decisions.

The military organization corresponds to the Barbarian stage in our life cycle model. But the more the organization moves up the curve, the more the decision-making process must be delegated. The Synergistic organization is highly collaborative with managers involved in team decisions at every level. This requires immediate performance feedback and scorekeeping by each team.

The systems of compensation and benefits in most organizations are based on the idea that there are vertical classes requiring differentiation. Stock options are provided for senior managers and not for lower-level employees. Why? Obviously we value managers at higher levels more than employees, and we want people to strive to move "upward." But why not offer stock options for employees who progress laterally, people who improve their skills or improve performance within one layer of the organization? Don't we value this, too?

Similarly, profit sharing has traditionally been designed for the upper classes of our minisociety on the assumption that profits stemmed from decisions made by managers and not from employees who were merely following orders. Is that assumption still true? Such a system teaches employees that they are not responsible for

TRADITIONAL MANAGEMENT STRUCTURE

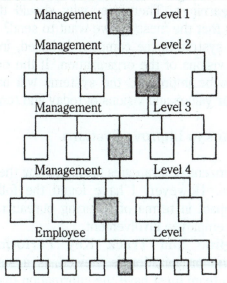

Management   Level 1

Management   Level 2

Management   Level 3

Management   Level 4

Employee   Level

TEAM MANAGEMENT STRUCTURE

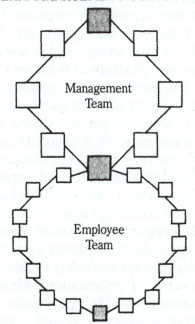

Management
Team

Employee
Team

producing earnings. Therefore, why should they try to improve margins? Is that the message we want to send?

Every system in the company is based, in some measure, on values and visions of the organization. If the organization's performance is to be improved, the systems will have to be realigned based on our values and visions of today and tomorrow.

Action Plans to Improve Systems

There are dozens of strategies for improving the systems that affect performance. However, I have found the following to have the greatest impact in terms of reducing bureaucracy and inertia and maximizing employee involvement.

1. Define and Track Key Performance for Every Team If the organization is viewed as a series of interlocking teams, each team must have the information that allows it to accept responsibility for its performance. Each team should meet on a regular basis to discuss and review how performance may be improved. In a manufacturing organization employee teams should meet at least weekly, some even once every day. Management teams at lower levels should meet weekly, higher levels less often.

2. Implement Statistical Process Control The Japanese success story has been explained in many ways. However, one technique, perhaps more than any other, can be credited with their superior quality. Statistical process control was introduced to the Japanese by the American, W. Edwards Deming. Statistical process control, or SPC, provides continuous monitoring of statistical variation in quality and graphic plotting of variability of products and services on "control charts" and establishes the basis for employee problem solving, or continuous improvement.

This method requires considerable training and creates a very different philosophy about the management of performance. There is a shift from blaming and controlling to analyzing and correcting.

3. Implement Performance Management Methods Performance management, like SPC, teaches managers to be more systematic in their attempts to improve performance. This method is based on the use of behavioral psychology, particularly the principles of positive reinforcement, behavior shaping, and feedback. Each manager should develop action plans to improve performance and systematically reward those improvements.

4. Redesign the Total System The most comprehensive way to address the question of whether systems are helping to create synergy is to redesign the entire organization. The redesign calls for all systems to be put aside and new ones created as the new design requires. This is a "zero-based" systems approach. It has the advantage of potentially eliminating all systems that are viewed as sacred cows.

I was recently involved in a comprehensive redesign process at Moody's Investor Services, publishers of Moody's Manuals. The design teams comprised of first-level employees and managers created a total system for judging skills and rewarding performance based upon training, competency, and promotions. The design teams expected their compensation plan would be rejected by the steering committee because it included raises for most employees. They justified these raises on the increased levels of responsibility and skill required to perform the new jobs they created as part of the redesign. To their surprise, the steering committee, which included the division human resources manager, accepted their proposal and even considered the raises conservative. The redesign resulted in a 30 percent increase in productivity and the creation of several new products creating new revenues.

Skills

As companies mature, skills become more specialized. At the beginning of the life cycle all soldiers make their own swords and shields. Soon there are specialized sword and shield manufacturers, and before long each manufacturer has separate engineering, production, and research departments. With a continued dedication to specialization, it is predictable that the coordination between these departments will soon break down, and they will pursue conflicting paths, wasting energy and resources and reducing the competitiveness of the organization.

Many of our modern organizations suffer from overspecialization. This illness is common both at the top and bottom. Executives at the top may know only finance and not understand production or marketing. At the bottom, the work is so fragmented that workers can't feel any pride in the final product.

In the mature corporation, it is also likely there will be a shift from the functional skills of product innovation, producing, and selling to the support skills of finance, planning, and personnel. The bulk of American industry in recent years has suffered from a shift in emphasis from the primary skills to support skills.

An employee's skills will affect the way he deals with people. Several years ago I worked with the Honeywell Aerospace and Defense Group. Almost all of the managers were engineers who grew up in the organization developing three-ring laser gyroscopes and other high-technology products. When I interviewed these managers and asked them for their impressions of their colleagues, they would frequently accuse another manager of being "binary."

"Binary" is a term common among electrical engineers. "Being expressed by using only two digits, 0 and 1," is the way *Webster's* explains it.

Engineers have a tendency, generalized from their technical work, to see things as either right or wrong, black or white, 0 or 1. But as valued as it may be in engineering, when applied to judgments about people, it represents a problem. Colleagues, and customers, have an annoying habit of coming in shades of gray.

Action Steps to Improve the Skills in Your Organization

Most senior executives are so concerned with the financial reports of yesterday's performance that they give almost no attention to developing the potential of their employees—the people upon whom the company's future depends. This is both cause and symptom of the corporation in decline.

1. Develop an Ethic of Continual Improvement The best companies believe in continual improvement. For example, we may be the best producer of cellular telephone equipment today, but we know that we must be even better tomorrow, and we are passionately focused on that challenge. Employees have a disciplined pursuit of personal competence—through continuing education—that never ends until the day they retire. Those companies and cultures that are healthy are characterized by continual learning and discovery. Those in decline know all the answers.

2. Cross-Train at Every Level An ethic of continual improvement is exemplified not only by providing the best-possible training in a specific job, but by ensuring all employees are cross-trained in complementary skills and jobs. This cross-training increases organizational flexibility, improves problem-solving skills, and enhances the self-esteem of all employees.

3. Celebrate Technical Achievement and Achievers We reward that which is important. We place medals on war heroes and athletes. We have Emmys, Oscars, and Tonys. We have MVPs and Hall of Famers. There is a good chance that you can name last year's winners of many of these awards. But can you name the winner of your company's engineering award? The innovation award? Why can't you name them? The answer is, they are not important! Or so our culture is teaching us.

Style

The character of day-to-day interactions among the members of an organization is the organization's style. Although the style of managers is inevitably linked to their skills, it is also tied to the company structure and systems and even the physical environment in which the work takes place.

Our firm was recently hired by a foundry in Monongahela, Pennsylvania. The workers melted scrap iron and poured the molten liquid—with sparks flying—into huge molds to form castings often weighing several tons. The heat of summer, or the cold of the Pennsylvania winter, blows through the large sheds that house the furnaces. This is a loud, dirty, and dangerous place. The men are strong. They stand like soot-covered statues, with blackened muscles and bulging arms, ready to pull, lift, and push the mass that is the product of their work. Their speech is direct, and they will say exactly how they feel with an emotional force that is as honest as their work.

In this foundry there had been a virtual war between management and labor, and more recently within the ranks of the workers themselves. When I first visited this plant, the workers glared at me and each other with distrust and anger.

The corporate climate of manufacturing plants, whether chemical, steel, or coal, in the mountain region of western Pennsylvania and West Virginia is the worst of any in the United States. The fierce sense of independence and antiauthoritarianism combined with a history of adversarial managers have produced a self-reinforcing cycle of animosity.

In the Monongahela foundry, our consultant was training the managers in praising employees and giving feedback. The first time one employee was praised for doing a good job he became so angry that he filed a grievance, claiming the supervisor was making fun of him. Unfortunately, praise was so deviant from the normal style of interaction between managers and workers that it was completely misinterpreted. This management style would only change gradually, as the structure and systems gave way to the new culture. After a year of training, the culture changed dramatically as the employees recognized their common interest with managers.

Steve Jobs, co-founder and former chairman of Apple Computer, sat in on a sales pitch to Apple managers by a well-known and respected training firm. Their pitch was particularly polished. The presenters brought brochures and statistics, four-color panels, and videotapes demonstrating what they would do. At its conclusion, Jobs stood up and said, "I have just one thing to say. . . ." at which point he placed his finger down his throat, bent over holding his stomach, and made a loud barfing sound as he exited the room. Witness the clash of style.

Style has significant effect on an organization's ability to make effective decisions, motivate employees, and bring about unified action. The style of managers can be clearly seen in the group decision-making process. One manager with whom I worked claimed to be a great advocate of participative decision making. In group meetings he would proclaim loudly that he wanted everyone to speak his mind and that "this is a group decision." But none of his managers ever believed him. When I observed his behavior in a meeting, I found out why. When he stated his opinion he did so with an intimidating tone of voice, one that signaled to everyone in the room that there was only one right decision. His style stifled the participative process.

Action Plans to Improve Management Style

Management style is not improved by sending managers to "charm school." It is only improved when a new style of management leads to promotions that are tied to improvements in organizational performance. The style characteristics of Synergistic managers cannot be taught in isolation. They must be taught as a component of a "new way of managing."

1. Team Leadership Training Managers must be taught the skills of collaborative decision making and leading groups toward consensus. Listening and conflict resolution skills are essential components of such training.

2. Promote the Company Man (or Woman) In years past there was much talk about the "company man." Every company with a strong and cohesive culture has some ideal of the company man, whether it is Buck Rogers at IBM or Steve Jobs at Apple.

For many years it was a fact of organizational life that the manager who got promoted at any auto or steel company would be tough in his dealings with people. He talked tough and made tough decisions. Obviously this taught a generation of managers to behave the same way.

In any corporate culture, those likely to be promoted will conform to some stereotypical ideal of the "company man." What is that ideal? Why not state it openly and with clarity? Why not state that the company's ideal manager will be one who increases the self-esteem of his or her employees?

3. Continual Appraisal and Feedback When a company is young and entrepreneurial, the senior managers will be so close to all the action that formal systems of performance appraisal and feedback won't be necessary. Not so in a mature company. Although it is true that managers should give frequent feedback to their subordinates without the requirement of a system, the truth is they won't. The discipline of a system that requires this feedback is necessary as the company proceeds up the life cycle curve. Appraisals and feedback should always include the way managers get things done as well as what they get done. Style matters. It impacts the commitment, loyalty, and satisfaction of employees. Be certain your appraisal includes an evaluation—plus structured feedback—on management style.

4. Constant Example by Senior Executives Why does Charley Moritz, chairman of the Dun & Bradstreet Corporation, hold informal breakfast meetings with first-level employees every month? Why does he personally visit customers of his twenty-eight business units just to ask them if there is any way in which D&B services could be improved? It is not because he intends to directly affect those employees or customers. This, of course, may happen. But the real purpose is to show the thousands of other D&B managers the value of listening to employees and customers. This is behavior he wants all of his subordinates to engage in. And rather than just tell them to do it, he has decided to show them. Leaders lead by example. Whether Charles Moritz or Alexander the Great, true leaders have always understood that the best way to affect the behavior of subordinates is to serve as an example. This is particularly true in changing management style.

Symbols

As corporate managers, we value our rational judgment and behavior. We look down upon other cultures with their rituals and symbolic gestures. Yet if we could see ourselves through the eyes of an archaeologist one thousand years hence, we would gain quite a different perspective.

Picking through the ruins of a once tall office building, our future archaeologist might find strange pieces of cloth tied around the necks of each male who was surrounded by other symbols of the decision-making class. (He knew who was of that class by the size and furnishings of their private offices.) Because those who made decisions wore this piece of cloth, our archaeologist might attempt to develop a theory that this was used to signal agreement or disagreement with a decision. Perhaps he might theorize that it was slung over one shoulder to signal approval and the other to signal disapproval. Surely knowing what high intelligence and objectivity we had developed, he would assume that it had some functional value. Would he believe that the members of this superior class awoke each morning to place this ornament around their necks with no explanation or awareness of their strange behavior?

We employ all sorts of symbols in ritualistic fashion and, like the inhabitants of other cultures, give little thought to their origin or their impact on behavior. We have separate parking and entrances for managers and employees. Why? To send a message that managers are different from, superior to, and more important than employees. Why do we want to send this message? Mr. Irimajiri, president of Honda Manufacturing, sits at his desk in Marysville in a large open room with dozens of others, of every rank, all dressed alike in a white uniform. The reason for this is more symbolic than functional. The message clearly is that everyone at Honda is valued equally. Honda does not seem to have suffered as a result of these nontraditional symbols.

Symbols are generally not important by themselves. Whether the president of Honda has a private office or not, whether there are separate parking places for employees and managers, has little impact on the bottom line. But the messages those symbols send are important.

In the southern United States not too many years ago there were separate water fountains marked "White" and "Colored." The same water flowed into each. Some asked, "What's the big deal?" The symbolic message had another meaning: the two races must not mingle.

Action Plans to Create Symbols of Synergy

As companies mature and become increasingly complex, the levels of management increase, as do the barriers between those making important decisions and those who do the work. The reason to break down these barriers has nothing to do with motivating or appeasing employees. It must be done to keep the executives in touch with reality, how the work is being done, and why customers are satisfied or dissatisfied. The quality of leadership and decision making is dependent upon this connection.

1. Senior Executives Must Communicate with Workers and Customers The direct communication between workers and managers is important, not just because of the information passed, but also as a symbol that executives value and trust employees. Everyone in the company should know that those at the top listen to and care about those at the bottom. It is the responsibility of management to assure this is the case.

2. Rewards Based on Performance are Desirable; Those Based on Class Breed Contempt Cultures that value performance reward performance. The first duke won his parcel of land because he led a cavalry charge and the prince rewarded his valor with property. The tenth-generation heirs of this duke, now also dukes, possess the same parcel of land but now only lead the fox hunt charge. Companies develop the bad habit of offering high levels of pay, perks, and profits to those who are sitting in the seat of power rather than to those who are producing.

When the executive is giving a speech to employees, does he mention the names of engineers who made a manufacturing breakthrough? Does he praise employees or employee teams who set quality or production records last month? He should, if he wants to show the staff what the company believes to be important.

3. Open Environment, Open Communication, Open Mind The open office environment described earlier at Honda is symbolic of open communications. The manager who makes himself available is saying to his employees that he believes they are important, that he wants to listen. One manufacturing plant I know has a coded lock between the plant area and the managers' offices, and only managers know the code. Immediately inside the door is a kitchenette with free coffee and drinks for the managers. Secretaries are instructed to police the kitchen to make sure employees do not take the free drinks. After all, they have their own canteen with vending machines. These are symbols of the disconnection between managers and workers.

4. Sell the Artwork It was once assumed that people would do business with you if you looked like a successful company. If your offices were adorned with expensive artwork, the assumption went, your company was successful. Those days are dead! We know too well that the funds spent for artwork are funds not paid out in stockholder dividends, depleting shareholder value. We know that the time and effort executives spend in the construction of new office buildings is a distraction from improving the quality of their products. A modest appearance, comfortable yet not plush, gives a far better impression of corporate success and responsibility today. Sell the artwork and spend the money on manufacturing technology!

Responding to the Environment

No culture is an island. The corporation suffers constant pounding from the waves of technological change, political and economic swings, and shifting social norms. It is useless to view the managers of a corporation as the sole determinant of their corporate culture when forces far beyond their control can blow away their best plans and intentions.

Technological changes are forcing shifts in the culture of virtually every corporation. The company president carries a laptop computer and, from his hotel room at night, taps into the company computer to receive not only his messages, but the daily reports from each of his twenty-six manufacturing plants. He then plots on a graph so he can compare performance over the last twelve months. Previously, the president received this kind of data once a quarter, and dozens of highly paid managers spent days or weeks preparing it. Now he receives it instantly in his hotel room one thousand miles away.

The day is rapidly approaching when every employee will directly access and input information into the computer and will have immediate access to all significant information. What change will this produce?

It will produce management efficiency: fewer managers will handle more data. With more immediate information, employees at every level will be better able to solve problems. The improved flow of information will increase creativity and improve problem solving.

Technology will also affect the marketplace in which the company competes. Technology is changing so rapidly that increasing numbers of companies will be caught in technological market traps. The entire semiconductor industry slumped recently. Part of the problem was caused by foreign competition. But only part of it. The industry's rapid growth made it impossible to predict growth accurately. As a result, supply rapidly exceeded demand.

Companies are constantly making predictions about the economy, and those predictions affect the corporate culture. Allan Krowe, IBM's chief financial officer, had predicted a continuing 15 percent growth in IBM's market and its business. He was wrong—on both counts. Both the size of the market and IBM's earnings fell. In October 1986 Krowe was reassigned, and IBM reorganized and reduced staff through early retirement incentives.

The political environment is continually producing shocks to the corporation. Equal Employment Opportunity laws, liability laws, tax changes, the defense budget, and industry deregulation are all political decisions that affect the beliefs and behavior of employees.

Consider what has happened to AT&T. Every couple of months hundreds of thousands of jobs change, based on the decisions of one man, Judge Harold Greene, who is overseeing the breakup of "Ma Bell." Given this uncertainty, how entrepreneurial can AT&T, or any of the "baby Bells," be?

The social environment exerts control both through market forces and the pool from which employees are drawn. Every consumer marketing organization constantly has its ear to the ground trying to sense changes in the social environment that may alter buying patterns. Are people becoming more or less health conscious? How do they feel today about smoking? Alcohol? Their feelings affect not only sales, but the self-esteem of the employees who produce those products.

Where businesses choose to locate is largely the result of social forces. American Express moved a major financial information center from downtown Manhattan to Utah primarily because of the stronger work ethic there. Management-union relations in some places are so bad that companies avoid them. Why not locate in Smyrna, Tennessee, where employees do not assume the company is out to get them? Just as employees want to trust their company, management wants to be trusted and to trust its employees.

A company's culture, while largely controlled by management, cannot be divorced from the external influences of technology, the economy, politics, and the social environment. Management cannot change these forces, but it must respond to them. In the past the culture of an organization was viewed as something immovable. Today the culture of every corporation is constantly changing from one life cycle stage to the next, responding to the challenge of foreign competition and new market conditions.

This is the most exciting and, I believe, most desirable time ever to be managing in a corporation. Why? Because when dynamic conditions exist, competitive advantage can be quickly gained or lost. This is a time when you can influence the culture and direction of your organization. An inert object is difficult to direct. An object in motion will change direction with just slight pressure to one side or the other.

There is one final reason why this is the most desirable time to be a corporate manager. When historians look back on the last quarter of the twentieth century, they will see it represented the most revolutionary change in mankind's conduct of business. It will be seen as a period of collective synergy and interdependence. For thousands of years it has been assumed that to achieve spiritual progress, one had to be detached from the pursuit of the material. The holy men of the past went to the desert to demonstrate their detachment from the material. The merchant trading in the bazaar and the lender of money was assumed to be morally corrupt. Perhaps this was true in our immaturity. But we are entering a day in which all things are made new, and among them will be the relationship between the material and spiritual.

The task confronting every leader in every organization is to create a culture in which the creation of wealth is successfully pursued, but in a manner that enhances the spiritual progress of all its members. This is the challenge.

A Life Cycle Overview

STAGE 1: THE PROPHETIC AGE

The Business Environment The business is just getting started and may consist of one product and one customer, or the business is just entering a period of major renewal. The product (or service) is probably unique but crudely developed. Financially the company is probably in debt and living from month to month, hoping to cover the bills. The Prophet may be looking for investors or other financial help.

What Prophets Believe Prophets hold, and can usually engender in others, a strong, determined faith in the new product or service. The idea, and a vision of its potential, is their focus. The founder usually has a set of principles around which he wants to form his company. Prophets believe these principles set them apart. They and their followers have very high standards and the capacity for sacrificial effort. They are not likely to believe in the ability of others outside their small group.

Mission and Task Their task is to create the idea of a product or service. It is not important to Prophets whether they are fully capable of seeing it to its fulfillment. Their vision is their most important product. They also create a basic set of values that form the basis of the company's culture.

Style of Management The Prophet makes decisions by himself. He may share ideas and may listen to others, but he is not likely to participate or lead consensus decision making well. He will probably not follow up on decisions because he has little patience with details. Prophets have too many ideas and sometimes drive subordinates crazy with half-baked concepts that they expect others to follow to completion.

Organization What organization? The Prophet will be the first to violate his own organization. It is not important to him. Often he doesn't understand structures and systems, and he is likely to see them as constraints that he will all too happily go around, shake off, or change on a whim.

STAGE 2: THE BARBARIAN AGE

The Business Environment Cash flow is improving, but the company is still living in debt. Any would-be profit is being plowed back into development and expansion. The new company has established a base of customers and is highly focused on serving them and developing its product or service. It is making no effort to diversify or broaden its base.

What the Barbarian Believes The Barbarian believes in the Prophet's idea or creation and feels that its success rests entirely in his own hands. The Barbarian believes that he is in a life-or-death struggle to accomplish the early objectives of the organization.

Mission and Tasks To get the product to market and establish its acceptance.

The Barbarian Style High control and direct action. He will be on the field himself, carrying the banner, leading the troops into battle. It's get on his team or get out of the way.

Organization Simple structure, few if any systems. Few vertical layers and few horizontal differentiations. Non-Bureaucratic, highly personal. People may do more than one job; there is a high degree of flexibility; and deep loyalties to the heroic figure of the past.

STAGE 3: THE BUILDING AND EXPLORING AGE

The Business Environment The company is now showing a profit. However, large sums of capital are needed to exploit the opportunities for growth. The company may go public during this period. The organization is also strong enough to begin diversifying.

What Builders and Explorers Believe The Builder believes in the product and the means of production. He believes the value of the business is its ability to produce efficiently. He believes in the techniques, equipment, and people who have their hands on the product and equipment.

The Explorer believes in the product or service, but his belief is more focused on the potential for expansion. The Explorer is the manager most in touch with the customer and most concerned about how the company and its products are viewed externally. The Explorer is also the most competitive manager in the organization and very conscious of how the company is doing against its competition.

Their Mission and Task The mission of the Builder is to create efficient means of production. During this period of expansion, he is under pressure to produce more, yet he is constantly struggling to maintain quality and efficiency.

The mission of the Explorer is to conquer the potential market and build the most efficient means of selling.

Their Style of Management The Builder is a detail person. He wants to know exactly how things will be done. He walks around his plant talking to people about the work they are doing, and he probably knows as much or more about the production process as anyone. He is concerned with the numbers from yesterday, today, and tomorrow. He is not focused on longer-term plans.

The Explorer's management is based largely on interpersonal relationships. He is enthusiastic and loves opportunities to express his enthusiasm. He is intuitive. He wants to establish one-on-one relationships with clients but is frustrated with the lack of time his growing business leaves him to do it. He does no managing, and he hates paperwork.

Their Organization The organizations of both the Builder and Explorer are rapidly growing during this phase. They are beginning to develop specializations, causing the early stages of internal competition. During this stage the greatest burden is to grow without making significant and costly errors that will hinder the company in the future.

STAGE 4: THE ADMINISTRATIVE AGE

The Business Environment The company has entered a stage of business security in which it has mastered its primary market, has built up substantial assets, is making a respectable profit, and has a positive cash flow. It is investing in expanding secondary markets and is probably splitting into a divisional structure based on product segments. It is known and respected for its primary business but is looking for recognition in a broader market.

What the Administrator Believes The Administrator believes in efficiency. He believes that it is his job to maximize the financial success of the company. He believes that financial results will be improved by perfecting management systems and practices and by sound financial management. He believes in the company's products or services, but he takes them for granted. He spends little time with either production or marketing activities.

Mission and Tasks To maximize the efficiency of structures and systems and the use of financial resources.

Style of Management The Administrator may try to maintain the more consultative style of the Builder, Explorer, and Synergist, but he is not as effective in dealing with people. He would rather make decisions based on the facts. He will spend much of his time in search of the "correct" facts to provide the "correct" answers. He will order many studies.

Organization The Administrator is successful in that the organization probably operates most smoothly and efficiently during his tenure. Because he believes that the solution to problems can be found in organization and systems, both expand during the Administrative Age. More levels of management to control are added. Line managers are loosing power, staff is gaining power.

STAGE 5: THE BUREAUCRATIC AGE

The Business Environment The business is now diversified. The primary business is now viewed as a "cash cow," a steady producer of reasonable profits, but slow growth. The company is now acquiring younger businesses in search of faster growth and higher margins. It is also trying to improve margins by cost cutting.

What the Bureaucrat Believes The Bureaucrat believes in "professional management." He believes there is nothing wrong with the organization that sound management, defined as sound financial management and effective controls, cannot repair. Other ills can be corrected by acquiring or divesting assets. Other than through cost reduction, he does not believe he can have any particular impact on the viability of business units. He believes in strategic planning, comprising financial analysis and assumptions about the future productivity of assets based on passive, noncreative assumptions about the people who represent those assets.

Their Mission and Task The Bureaucrat is probably a former Administrator, and he still views his mission as making the structures and systems effective and managing the assets of the corporation with an eye toward boosting return on equity. He does not understand that this return is based on creativity that he is now stifling. His external focus is directed less at customers and suppliers and more at stock analysts and board members.

The Bureaucratic Style The Bureaucrat tends to be impersonal, more concerned with numbers than people. He likes written reports and responds to well-written reports. The paper flow increases as a result. The Bureaucrat is usually polite, although he can be provoked to autocratic outrage. As the Bureaucratic Age progresses, the Bureaucrat's tendency to autocratic command increases as his frustration with the ineffectiveness of his actions builds.

Organization The Bureaucrat considers his company to be "well organized," and it is, if that means many well-defined layers and clear delineations of responsibility. It is also overorganized, excessively layered with too many highly specialized groups. As the company grows it becomes more difficult to get decisions made. Quality information becomes unlikely to reach the top, and trust between managers and employees breaks down.

STAGE 6: THE ARISTOCRATIC AGE

The Business Environment The primary business of the organization is declining because of the lack of investment and creativity. The leaders have spent their resources on the acquisition of new businesses, have built up the debt, and have proceeded to impose their culture on the acquisitions, thwarting their development. Profit is now stagnant, the stock price declining. The company is divesting business units to produce cash.

What the Aristocrat Believes Aristocrats are increasingly victims of the cynicism that is overcoming the entire organization. They do believe in the attainment of personal wealth, and they are most likely to accomplish this through deal making of some sort. They seek personal satisfaction in the symbols of success.

Their Mission and Task Their primary mission is to prevent the further erosion of the company caused by creative individuals leaving to seek more supportive environments.

Their Management Style They are aloof. They rarely say very much of substance. They find it difficult to make decisions and have delegated most, if not all, of the operating decisions. When confronted with a situation in which they must make a decision, they are likely to resort to a highly autocratic style.

Organization The organization is characterized by excessive layers of management, poor communication from top to bottom, little clarity of mission, and poor motivation. Various sorts of internal warfare, competition among fiefdoms, is likely to be rampant. There is a clear formal organization, but that is not how things get accomplished. There is an informal organization used by those managers who are still genuinely interested in getting something done.

Notes and References

Introduction

1. Oswald Spengler, *The Decline of the West*, Volume 1 (New York: Alfred A. Knopf, 1926), p. 106.

2. Paul Kennedy, *The Rise and Fall of the Great Powers* (New York: Random House, 1987), p. xv.

3. Arthur Schlesinger, *The Cycles of American History* (Boston: Houghton Mifflin Company, 1986), p. 27.

4. Arnold Toynbee, *A Study of History*, Volume 7B (New York: Oxford University Press, 1962), p. 423.

Stage 1

1. Spengler, *The Decline of the West*, p. 106.

2. Robert Conot, *Thomas A. Edison: A Streak of Luck* (New York: Da Capo, 1979), p. 455.

3. P. R. Nayak and J. M. Ketteringham, *Breakthroughs!* (New York: Rawson Associates, 1986), pp. 15–17.

4. Toynbee, *A Study of History*, Volume 11, p. 259.

5. John F. Love, *McDonald's—Behind the Arches* (New York: Bantam Books, 1986), p. 14.

6. Ken Auletta, *The Art of Corporate Success* (New York: Penguin Books, 1985), pp. 17–25.

7. Peter Drucker, *Innovation & Entrepreneurship: Practices & Principles* (New York: Harper & Row, 1985), p. 19.

8. George Gilder, *The Spirit of Enterprise* (New York: Simon & Schuster, 1984), p. 102.

9. Lucien Rhodes, "Kuolt's Complex" (*Inc.*, April 1986), pp. 72–84.

Stage 2

1. John Keegan, *The Mask of Command* (New York: Viking, 1987), p. 11.

2. Lee Iacocca, *Iacocca: An Autobiography* (New York: Bantam Books, 1984), pp. 155–57.

3. Jerome Carcopino, *Daily Life in Ancient Rome* (New Haven: Yale University Press, 1966), pp. 238–43.

4. Edward Gibbon, *The Decline and Fall of the Roman Empire*, Volume 2 (New York: The Modern Library), p. 248.

5. Ibid., p. 252.

6. Keegan, *The Mask of Command*, p. 91.

7. Mary Renault, *The Nature of Alexander* (New York: Pantheon Books, 1975), p. 92.

8. Ibid., p. 93.

9. Ibid., p. 127

10. H. G. Wells, *The Outline of History* (Garden City, New York: Doubleday & Company, Inc., 1971), p. 307.

11. Michael Moritz, *The Little Kingdom* (New York: William Morrow & Company, 1984), p. 95.

12. Peter Petre, "What Welch Has Wrought at GE" (*Fortune*, July 7, 1987).

Stage 3

1. Samuel Eliot Morison, *The Great Explorers* (New York: Oxford University Press, 1978), p. 427.

2. Edward G. Bourne, quoted in Morison, *The Great Explorers*, p. 556.

3. David Howarth, *The Voyage of the Armada: The Spanish Story* (New York: Viking, 1981), p. 23.

4. Gary Jacobson and John Hillkirk, *Xerox: The American Samurai* (New York: MacMillan Publishing Company, 1986), p. 58.

5. Ibid., p. 5.

6. Ibid., p. 26.

7. Paul R. Lawrence and Jay W. Lorsch, *Organization and Environment* (Boston: Harvard Business School Press, 1969), p. 108.

8. Toynbee, *A Study of History*, Volume 3, p. 143.

Stage 4

1. Alfred Chandler, Jr., *The Visible Hand* (Cambridge, Massachusetts: The Belknap Press of Harvard University Press, 1977), p. 83.

2. Ibid., p. 102.

3. Ibid., p. 104.

4. Ibid., p. 147.

5. Wells, *The Outline of History*, pp. 385–86.

6. Ibid., p. 408

7. F. W. Farrar, in Wells, *The Outline of History*, p. 408.

8. Robert H. Hayes, "Strategic Planning—Forward in Reverse?" (*Harvard Business Review*, November-December 1985), pp. 111–19.

9. David K. Hurst, "Why Strategic Management Is Bankrupt" (*Organizational Dynamics*, Autumn 1986, American Management Association, New York), pp. 16–20.

10. Ibid., pp. 8–9.

11. Ibid., p. 10.

12. Ibid., p. 11.

13. Toynbee, *A Study of History*, Volume 4, p. 130.

14. Peter Drucker, *The Frontiers of Management* (New York: Truman Talley Books, E. P. Dutton, 1986), pp. 257–59.

Stage 5

1. *Wall Street Journal*, November 7, 1986, p. 19.

2. Gibbon, in Toynbee, *A Study of History*, Volume 4, p. 63.

3. Wells, *The Outline of History*, p. 409.

4. Ibid., p. 419.

5. Toynbee, *A Study of History*, Volume 4, p. 5.

6. Hedrick Smith, *The Russians* (New York: Ballantine Books, 1976), p. 289.

7. Arkady N. Shevchenko, *Breaking with Moscow* (New York: Alfred A. Knopf, Inc., 1985), p. 79.

8. Ibid., p. 489.

9. Robert J. Schoenberg, *Geneen* (New York: Warner Books, 1985), p. 63.

10. Ibid., p. 63.

11. Ibid., p. 73.

12. Ibid., p. 202.

13. Ibid., p. 204.

14. Robert Heller, *The Naked Manager—Games Executives Play* (New York: Truman Talley Books, E. P. Dutton, 1985), p. 268.

15. Toynbee, *A Study of History*, Volume 5, p. 17.

Stage 6

1. Drucker, *The Frontiers of Management*, p. 180.

2. *Fortune*, February 1988.

3. Ibid.

4. Barbara W. Tuchman, *The March of Folly* (New York: Ballantine Books, 1984), p. 75.

5. Ibid., p. 90.

6. Adam Smith, "Unconventional Wisdom" (*Esquire*, February 1986), p. 75.

7. Arnold Toynbee, *A Study of History*, Abridgement by D. C. Somervell (New York: Dell Publishing, 1965), p. 419.

Stage 7

1. Love, *McDonald's—Behind the Arches*, p. 114.

2. Ibid., p. 88.

3. Ibid., p. 100.

4. Lucien Rhodes, "The Turnaround" (*Inc.*, August 1986), pp. 42–48.

5. Stephen R. Covey, *Seven Habits of Highly Successful People*, unpublished manuscript.

Index

accounting, 121–123, 177
achievement awards, 207, 212
acquisitions, corporate, 81
  Administrators and, 94–95, 102–105, 106,
    107–108
  Aristocrats and, 152–153, 154, 163, 164
  Bureaucrats and, 111, 115–116, 121, 124–127
  diversification through, 103–104, 107–108,
    126–127
Adams, John, 11, 160
administrations, 80–81, 177, 186–188
Administrators, 46, 56, 83–109, 121, 132, 154,
  182, 219–220
  acquisitions and, 94–95, 102–105, 106,
    107–108
  beliefs of, 219–220
  in business, 92–96, 219
  character of, 85–89
  corporate socialism and, 106–108
  cost reduction by, 100–102
  creativity and, 105–106
  customer-focused, 108–109
  in history, 89–92
  leadership vs management and, 84
  management style of, 220
  organizations of, 97–100, 220
  quality control by, 100–102
  staff increased by, 99–100
  stockholders and, 106–107
  strategic planning and, 93–96, 101
  tasks of, 100–109, 220
  work relationships with, 96–97
airlines, 32, 47, 49–50, 60, 161, 189–190,
  193, 195
Alexander the Great, 40, 42–46, 57, 60,
  174, 198
Alexander VI, Pope, 150–151
Allen-Bradley Company, 134
American Railroad Journal, 87
American Restaurant Magazine, 21
Apple Computer, 26–27, 30, 47–48, 179,
  208, 209
Araskog, Rand V., 127
Aristocrats, 106, 139–164, 221–222
  acquisitions and, 152–153, 154, 163, 164
  beliefs of, 222
  in business, 152–155, 221–222
  character of, 141–147
  competition and, 161–162
  customers and, 161–162
  definition of, 141
  employees vs , 159–161
  in history, 147–152
  legitimacy of power and, 139–140
  management style of, 222
  organizations of, 156–158, 222
  rebellions against, 106, 140, 151–152,
    158–164
  stockholders and, 106, 162–164
  tasks of, 158–164, 222
  work relationships with, 155–156
Arrian, 44–45
artworks, symbolic value of, 212–213
Atari, 47
AT&T, 214
Attila the Hun, 36, 41–42, 46
auto industry, 101–102, 115, 140, 161, 166–
  173, 209
  see also specific companies
Aztecs, 147–149

Baha'u'llah, 165
banking industry, 140
Barbarians, 22, 31, 34–58, 62, 76, 83, 86, 99,
  118, 121, 124, 129, 135, 154, 182, 202,
  217–218
  beliefs of, 217–218
  in business, 46–50, 217
  character of, 36–40
  complacency vs challenges of, 57–58
  concepts actualized by, 55–56
  corporate cultures and, 56
  customers and, 53
  discipline imposed by, 53–54
  flexibility maintained by, 53–54
  in history, 40–46
  insensitivity of, 56–57
  management style of, 218
  organizations of, 51–53, 218
  tasks of, 53–58, 218
  work relationships with, 50–51
Beard, Charles A , 157
Beatrice Foods, 140, 145–146
Becker, Horace, 69–70
Beecher, Henry Ward, 145

Beech-Nut Foods, 140
Bell & Howell, 121
Bendix, 145
Benedict, Saint, 19
Bennett, Harry, 61
Best Foods, 199
Bethlehem Steel, 137, 140, 157
boards of directors, 112–113, 162–163
Borman, Frank, 195
Bourne, Edward G , 65
Boylan, Dick, 183
Breakthroughs! (Nayak and Ketteringham),
    14–15
Bremer, Brian, 133
Brezhnev, Leonid, 114
British Empire, 111–112, 200
Buddha, 16, 17, 19
Builders, 20, 46, 59–82, 83, 99, 118, 121, 154,
    218–219
  administrations and, 80–81
  beliefs of, 218
  in business, 69–72, 218
  character of, 61–64
  cost reductions and, 79
  Explorers vs , 62–63, 64–66, 73, 77, 80, 83,
    99, 118, 121, 154, 182, 218, 219
  in history, 64–68
  management style of, 77, 219
  marketing and, 70, 73, 79
  motivational conflicts and, 62–63
  organizations of, 73–78, 219
  overexpectations of, 81–82
  quality control and, 79
  specialized competence and, 79–80
  tasks of, 78–82, 218–219
  work relationships with, 72–73
bureaucracies, 29–30, 54, 70, 88
Bureaucrats, 25, 92, 110–138, 176, 220–221
  acquisitions and, 111, 115–116, 121, 124–127
  beliefs of, 220–221
  in business, 120–127, 220
  centralization of power by, 129, 136
  challenge and response of, 135
  character of, 111–114
  command decision making by, 129
  conditions of ease and, 135–136
  counterstructures fostered by, 132
  creativity and, 128, 134–135
  excess of specialization by, 130–132
  in history, 114–120

  machinelike behavior of, 130
  management style of, 221
  new leadership needed by, 133–134
  organizations of, 128–132, 221
  passive vs aggressive, 111–112
  resistance to change in, 119–120
  restructuring needed by, 136–137
  social unity and, 110, 126, 137–138
  strategic planning by, 118–119
  tasks of, 133–138, 221
  work relationships with, 127–128
Burr, Donald C , 60
Bushnell, Nolan, 47
business schools, 49, 53, 93, 101, 154–155

Carcopino, Jerome, 41
Carlson, Chester, 69, 70
Carter, Jimmy, 84
Carthage, 89–90
Castro, Fidel, 29
Chandler, Alfred D , Jr , 88
Chrysler Corporation, 37–38, 101, 166, 196
Columbus, Christopher, 63
command decision making, 36, 53, 78, 129, 189
communication, 126, 137–138, 212
company men, 209
Compaq computer, 179
competitive strategies, internal, 192–215
  achievement awards in, 207, 212
  artworks vs , 212–213
  communication in, 212
  company men and, 209
  conceptual frameworks in, 193–198
  cross-training in, 207
  external influences on, 180, 213–215
  improvement ethic in, 206–207
  leadership by example in, 210
  management styles in, 207–210
  open office environments in, 172, 211, 212
  performance management in, 202, 204–205,
    209–210, 212
  restructuring in, 200–201, 205
  senior executives and, 210, 212
  shared visions in, 194–198, 200, 204
  skills in, 205–207
  span of control in, 199–200, 201
  statistical process control in, 204
  structures in, 198–202
  symbols in, 210–213
  systems in, 202–205

team leadership training in, 209
teamwork in, 195, 196, 201–202, 204
computer industry, 26–27, 30, 47–48, 179–180, 208, 209
consensus decision making, 26, 77, 180, 189
Confucius, 19
Continental Airlines, 49
Continental Can Company, 103, 140, 152–154
Corning Glass Works, 133
corporate cultures, 56, 193–194
corporate socialism, 106–108
Cortes, Hernan, 147, 148–149
cost reductions, 79, 100–102, 111, 130, 150
counterstructures, 132
Covey, Stephen R , 190
Crassus, 90–91
Cray Research, 179
creativity, 105–106, 128, 134–135, 176–178
  see also Prophets
cross-training, 207
Cuba, immigrants from, 29
customers, 53, 76, 108–109, 131, 136, 161–162, 174, 175, 177
cycles, corporate, 1–8, 165, 216–222
Cycles of American History, The (Schlesinger), 4

Dana Corporation, 199, 200
DEC, 179
decentralization, 129, 183
decision making, 77–78
  command, 36, 53, 78, 129, 189
  consensus, 26, 77, 180, 189
  group, 77, 171, 208–209
  on-the-spot, 188–189
Declaration of Independence, 158–159
Decline and Fall of the Roman Empire (Gibbon), 40, 116
Decline of the West, The (Spengler), 10
Delta Airlines, 161, 189–190, 193, 195
Deming, W Edwards, 204
discipline systems, 170–171
divestitures, 134, 162, 163
Drake, Sir Francis, 67–68
Drucker, Peter, 27, 62, 103–104, 134, 139
Dun & Bradstreet Corporation, 102, 103, 195, 210
Du Pont, 201

ease, conditions of, 81, 97–98, 135–136, 174, 178, 184

Eastern Airlines, 49, 195
Edison, Thomas A , 10–11, 13, 174
E F Hutton, 141–143
Electronic Data Systems, 39–40
Elizabeth I, Queen of England, 66, 67
employees, 110, 128, 137, 159–161, 174, 176, 177, 178–179, 185, 188, 199–200
entrepreneurs, 22, 93, 106, 132, 179, 180
Erie Scientific Co , 133
Explorers, 62–63, 64–66, 73, 77, 80, 83, 99, 118, 121, 154, 182, 218, 219
Exxon, 116, 163

Farrar, F W , 91–92
Federal Express, 55–56, 93
feedback, 170, 208, 209–210
financial reporting, 187–188
Foman, Robert, 141–143
Ford, Henry, 11, 13, 21, 61
Ford Motor Company, 101, 166, 195–196, 200
Forstmann Little, 133, 134
Fortune, 141–142
Fox, Neil, 22
franchises, 21–22, 57, 181
Freeman, Lester, 29
Frito-Lay, 199
Frontier Airlines, 49

Garrett, David, 195
Gates, William, 30–31
Geneen, Harold, 120–127
General Electric Corporation, 10, 11, 54, 69
General Motors, 39, 40, 61, 101–102, 113, 138, 161, 166
Getty, J Paul, 9
Gibbon, Edward, 40, 41–42, 116
golden parachutes, 143, 145–146
Goldsmith, Sir James, 163
Gorbachev, Mikhail, 117, 119–120
Gramm-Rudman bill, 130
Greene, Harold, 214
Gregory, Saint, 19

Hadrian, Emperor of Rome, 91
Haloid Company, 69
Hawkyns, John, 67–68
Hayes, Robert H , 93
Healthdyne, Inc , 28–29
Hewlett-Packard, 177–178
Hicks, Wayland, 71–72

Honda of America Manufacturing, Inc , 102, 113,
135, 166–173, 174, 193, 195, 211, 212
Honeywell Aerospace and Defense Group, 206
Honeywell Corporation, 23–24
Horizon Air Industries, 32
housing industry, 124–129
Howard Johnson's, 162
Hurst, David K , 94, 95–96

Iacocca, Lee, 37–38, 196
IBM (International Business Machines), 27, 39,
48, 69, 70, 104, 162, 179, 193, 209, 214
Icahn, Carl, 152
immigrants, 29–30
Inc , 32–33
India, 111–112
Innocent VIII, Pope, 149–150
innovations, 14–15, 27–28, 67, 70, 90, 105,
134, 186
International Harvester Company, 187
Irimajiri, Shoichiro, 167–168, 169, 173, 211
iron foundries, 207–208
ITT, 120, 123–127, 137

Japan, 101–102, 113, 166, 170, 199, 204
Jarvis, Herbert W , 133
Jefferson, Thomas, 139, 146–147, 184
Jellinek, Frank H , Jr , 133
Jesus Christ, 16, 18–19, 135
Jobs, Steven, 30, 47–48, 208, 209
Johnson & Johnson, 27, 129
Jones & Laughlin Steel, 121–123
just-in-time inventory, 171

Kearns, David, 71, 198
Keegan, John, 37, 44
Kennedy, John F , 194
Kennedy, Paul, 3, 4
Ketteringham, J M , 14–15
Keynes, John Maynard, 13
Kiam, Victor, 34–35, 48
Krishna, 16, 19
Kroc, Ray, 20, 22, 36, 47, 48, 58, 180–183
Krowe, Allan, 214
Kuhn, Jim, 181
Kuolt, Milton G , II, 31–33

Lawrence, Paul R , 75–76
leadership, 46, 84, 93, 101, 110, 117, 133–134,
137, 144, 165, 174, 178–179, 210

Lenin, Nikolai, 19, 117–118
Leo X, Pope, 150
leveraged buy-outs, 133–134, 187
Levitt, Bill, 124–125
Lilienthal, David E , 128
Little Kingdom, The (Moritz), 47
L L Bean, 93
L M Ericsson, 123
Locke, John, 13
London, Jack, 175
Lorenzo, Frank, 47, 49–50, 195
Lorsch, Jay W , 75–76
Louis XIV, King of France, 144
Love, John F , 181–182
LSI, 124–126

MacArthur, Peter, 34
McCallum, Daniel C , 86–87
McDonald, Maurice (Mac), 20–22, 47
McDonald, Richard, 20–22, 47
McDonald's, 20–22, 36, 181–183
Magellan, Ferdinand, 64–66, 68, 174
Magenheim, Ellen B , 163
management styles, 31–33, 77, 136, 172,
207–210, 217, 218, 219, 220, 221, 222
Mao Tse-tung, 138
March of Folly, The (Tuchman), 149
Marcos, Ferdinand, 145
Marcus Aurelius, Emperor of Rome, 91–92
marketing, 70, 73, 79, 134, 166
Marquis de Lafayette Hotel, 145
Martino, June, 182
Marx, Karl, 117–118
Mask of Command, The (Keegan), 44
MBWA (management by walking around),
177–178
mergers, 86, 104, 111, 163–164
Merrill Lynch, 142
Metromedia, Inc , 104
Microsoft, Inc , 31
mill operating cost control (MOCC), 122
Minoans, 76
Mohammed, 16, 17–18, 19, 36
Montezuma II, 147, 148–149
Moody's Investor Services, 185–186,
199, 205
Moritz, Charley, 210
Moritz, Michael, 47
motorcycles, 169, 172
Motor Trend, 166

Mueller, Dennis C , 163
Murray, Jack, 103

Nature of Alexander, The (Renault), 45
Nayak, P R , 14–15
NEC (Nippon Electric Company), 123
Newton, Isaac, 12–13
Nixon White House syndrome, 153–154
NYNEX, 104–105

Patton, George S , IV, 38, 57
peer review, 170–171
People Express Airlines, 49, 60
Pepys, Samuel, 13
performance management, 99, 170–171, 202,
    204–205, 209–210, 212
Perot, H Ross, 39–40, 138
Petit, Pete, 28–29
Philip II, King of Spain, 66
popes, Renaissance, 149–152, 154, 162
Porsche, Dr , 19
positive reinforcement systems, 170
Principia (Newton), 12
prisons, 198–199
profit sharing, 170, 188, 202–204
Prophets, 9–33, 36, 46, 47, 61, 69, 99, 117–
    118, 124, 129, 135, 175, 176, 216–217
  beliefs of, 216–217
  bureaucracies vs , 29–30
  in business, 19–23, 216
  character of, 11–15
  in history, 16–19
  immigrants as, 29–30
  management style of, 31–33, 217
  mature corporations left by, 30
  new technology and, 30–31
  organizations of, 25–28, 217
  persecution of, 15, 25
  personal crises and, 28–29
  tasks of, 28–33, 217
  work relationships with, 24–25
Protestant Reformation, 149, 151

quality control, 79, 100–102, 161, 169, 170, 171,
    176, 183
quinqueremes, 89–90

racing, auto, 167–168
railroads, 85–88, 97
Raytheon, 123

Reagan, Ronald, 84, 109
Reliance Electric, 116, 163
religions, 16–19, 147–148, 149–152
Remington Shaver Corp , 34–35
Renault, Mary, 45
Revlon, 145
roads, decay of, 115
Rogers, Buck, 209
Rohatyn, Felix, 125
role models, 195–196
Roman Catholic Church, 149–152, 200
Roman Empire, 40–42, 89–92, 115, 116–117,
    126, 137, 200
Russelsteel Inc , 94–96
Russians, The (Smith), 118

Scherer, F Michael, 163
Schlesinger, Arthur M , 4
Schlumberger, 22–23
SCM, 70
Scythians, 91
semiconductor industry, 214
Seven Habits of Highly Successful People
    (Covey), 190
Shaw, George Bernard, 9
Shearson-American Express, 141, 214
Sherwin-Williams, 199
Shevchenko, Arkady N , 119–120
Simon, Paul, 191
Sixtus IV, Pope, 149
skills, 136, 171–172, 205–207
Sloan, Alfred P , 83
slogans, 161, 167, 190, 195, 196
Smith, Adam, 155
Smith, Fred, 55
Smith, Hedrick, 118
social unity, 110, 126, 137–138, 165–166, 175,
    180–184
Sonneborn, Harry, 182, 183
Southwestern Bell, 104, 202
Soviet Union, 114, 117–120, 160
Spanish Armada, 66–68
spans of control, 199–200, 201
specialization, 130–132, 205–206
    competence in, 79–80, 184–186
Spengler, Oswald, 3, 10
spirit, corporate, 174
Springfield Remanufacturing Center Corp ,
    187–188
Stack, John P , 187–188

Stalin, Joseph, 118
statistical process control, 204
statistics, 125–126
steel industry, 94–96, 121–123, 137, 140, 155, 157, 209
stockholders, 106–107, 113, 152, 162–164, 174, 213
stock options, 202
strategic planning, 93–96, 101, 118–119, 154–155
strikes, 160–161
structures, corporate, 99, 168–169, 198–202
  counterstructures vs , 132
  restructuring of, 98–99, 136–137, 160, 200–201, 205
styles, management, *see* management styles
Sudden Infant Death Syndrome (SIDS), 28–29
Sybron Corporation, 133–134
symbols, corporate, 113, 136, 172–173, 210–213
synergy, 84, 123, 134, 165–191, 215
  administrations in, 186–188
  axioms of, 5, 173–189
  balance sought by, 166, 177, 179
  challenge and response in, 178–179
  consensus in, 180, 189
  creativity in, 176–178
  definition of, 165
  diversity in, 180–184
  flexibility in, 173, 177, 186
  global, 190–191
  integration in, 184–186, 191
  management styles of, 172
  motivation in, 175, 178
  on-the-spot decisions in, 188–189
  planned urgency in, 179–180
  purpose in, 174–176, 186
  skills and, 171–172
  social unity created by, 165–166, 175, 180–184
  specialized competence in, 184–186
  spirit in, 174
  structures and, 168–169
  symbols and, 172–173, 211–213
  systems of, 170–171
  teamwork in, 172, 189–190, 195, 196
systems, corporate, 99, 136, 170–171, 202–205

takeovers, corporate, 152, 154
Taylor, Frederick, 199
team leadership training, 209
Texas Air Corporation, 47, 49–50
Thousand Trails, Inc., 31–32
Timberlake, John, 122–123
Toynbee, Arnold, 3, 7–8, 16, 57, 59, 76, 81, 98, 110, 115, 116, 137, 157
Toyota, 101–102, 200
Trajan, Emperor of Rome, 91
Tuchman, Barbara W , 149
Turner, Fred, 181, 182–183

Ueberroth, Peter, 143
unions, 88, 132, 161, 195
United Homes Corporation, 125
United States, 158–159, 191
  Congress of, 130
United States Steel, 137, 140, 155, 157
universities, 198–199
  business schools of, 49, 53, 93, 101, 154–55
  organization of, 74–75

Villard, Henry, 10

Wallas, Graham, 132
Wasserman, Dick, 125–126
Watson, Thomas, Sr , 83
Watt, James, 85
Weber, Max, 199
Welch, John F , Jr , 54
Wells, H G , 46, 90, 116–117
Westfall, Richard, 13
Wheelwright, Steven C , 101
Wian, Bob, 20
Wilson, Joe, 69, 70
Wilson, Woodrow, 144
Wozniak, Stephen, 11, 30, 47

Xerox: The American Samurai (Jacobson and Hillkirk), 72
Xerox Corporation, 48, 69–72, 102, 198, 200

Yontz, Kenneth F., 134
Young, John, 177–78

Zap Mail, 55–56
zero-based systems, 205